Contents

Acknowledgments

I WISH TO THANK Steve for his never-failing support and design of the figures in this book. Thanks also to David, Jonathan, Jake, and Ethan. They always make life interesting and help to keep me grounded. I would also like to thank the staff at Red Wheel/Weiser for their many contributions to this effort, especially Judika Illes, Tania Seymour, and Kathryn Sky-Peck.

In addition, I wish to thank the tarot teachers, writers, and students who have shared their insights and experiences with me over the years. You've added tremendously to my understanding. Finally, I offer my heartfelt gratitude to those everywhere who have felt inspired to look within for their Inner Guides. You are making a difference in the world.

Introduction

The tarot is a deck of seventy-eight picture cards that has been used for centuries to reveal hidden truths. In the past few years, interest in the tarot has grown tremendously. More and more people are seeking ways to blend inner and outer realities so they can live their lives more creatively. They have discovered in the tarot a powerful tool for personal growth and insight.

I have been studying the tarot for many years, and my focus has always been on how the cards can be used as a tool for inner guidance. In 1995, I created my online tarot course, and in 1998, my first book, *Learning the Tarot*, was published as a paperback. In 2021, I published my most comprehensive work, *The Big Book of Tarot*. This book you now hold in your hands addresses a very special and targeted subject area: tarot reversals. *Upside Down Tarot* is a concisely abridged reference book drawn from the coursework presented in *Learning Tarot Reversals*, which was published over twenty years ago. If you want to take your readings further and deeper, this easy-to-use reference guide is for you.

My experience with the cards is in doing readings for myself, friends, relatives, and acquaintances—probably the kind of tarot you are interested in. Learning to read the tarot is like putting together a puzzle—there are many pieces and many potential shapes. It's a juggling act for those who are learning to interpret the cards. Each card in a reading has layers of interpretation: meanings that come from keywords; archetypes; and even correspondences to astrology, numerology, qabbalah, and the elements of earth, air, fire, and water. If a card is in a spread, or pattern for laying out the cards, then the position the card falls in also adds meaning. The puzzle pieces combine to form a complete picture, shedding light on the seeker's question. When you examine these cards, you see how certain forces are impacting your life in the moment.

Any tarot deck you purchase will come with a "little white book"—a small pamphlet to teach you certain card meanings. Curious students then often want to learn more and go deeper. They seek out more comprehensive tarot books. To satisfy this desire, an abundance of beginner and how-to books have hit the market—good books that have introduced card meanings to so many who are ready to dive into the wisdom and insight the cards can offer. From the many excellent tarot books currently available, the tarot reader digests and internalizes card meanings, eventually adding their own intuitive understandings.

Sadly, many of these introductory books ignore or gloss over what to do when a card is upside down, or reversed. There is so much that can be said about the cards that reversals often get little or no attention. Turned upside down, tarot cards can have an entirely different meaning from their upright interpretations. Because of the lack of attention on reversals, they can be misunderstood. Some people interpret a reversed tarot card as showing bad news. Others think the reversed meaning must be the polar opposite of the upright meaning. And some ignore them completely, just flipping upright any card that has appeared upside down in a spread.

My approach to reversed cards is based on an appreciation of energies and their cycles. In our world, change is the one constant. A reading shows us forces that are not fixed but fluid and dynamic. The cards need to reflect this animated spirit if they are to mirror experience faithfully. How the cards are oriented—upright or reversed—is key to enhancing the energetic quality of a reading. In my system, when a card is reversed, its energy is not fully developed. It may be in its early stages or losing power. It may be incomplete or unavailable. The qualities of the card *are* present, at least in potential, but they can't express completely. When you look at reversals in this way, you enliven and deepen your tarot practice by adding a whole new dimension to it.

To truly reflect reality, a reading must capture life's movement and change. In this book, I describe how tarot reversals can enhance the dynamic quality of your readings by seeing your cards as energies. You'll discover how to translate a stationary set of images into a moving picture of time's flow. It's my hope that *Upside Down Tarot* will give you a new way to view your life experience and a more powerful tool for understanding it through your tarot readings.

How to Use This Book

In part one, I discuss the concept of reversed cards as energies. You'll learn how energies present in phases or cycles. Reversed card energies can be *absent*, *early* phase, or *late* phase. By understanding these concepts, you'll be able to make best use of the tarot card descriptions presented in part two.

Part one covers only the basics of card energy. Keep in mind that there is so much more to reading cards than just understanding the upright and reversed meanings! The cards relate to one another in so many complex and intriguing ways. For an in-depth guide on how to work with the cards in all their facets, I recommend reading *The Big Book of Tarot*, but for reversals, let *Upside Down Tarot* be your quick-reference guide.

Part One

THE
HIDDEN
MEANING
OF
REVERSALS

CHAPTER 1

Reversals Are Energy

Imagine a finished jigsaw puzzle. Looked at one way, it's a single object presenting a whole picture. Looked at another way, it's a collection of many objects—the pieces of the puzzle. The puzzle is *one* and *many* at the same time.

Now imagine the pieces moving and changing. The overall dimension of the puzzle stays the same, but the picture doesn't. It's recreated anew in every moment. Our universe is like this puzzle. It is a single entity but made up of countless changing "pieces." I call these pieces energies.

All living beings are energies, as are all inanimate objects. Qualities or states of being are also energies—the energy of love or despair can be a palpable force with a life of its own.

Energies often coalesce into groups to form larger energies. Each of us is such a group. Our bodies are made up of cells and organs; our personalities are traits and tendencies; our moods reflect thoughts, feelings, and desires. A person is a veritable energy vortex! Every minute of the day, energies of all kinds are flowing in, around, and through us. Some are mild, some strong. Some are new, some old. Some are welcome, some not so welcome. How does this energy flow relate to the tarot?

Every card in the tarot deck represents a certain energy. A card's energy is not its energy as a physical object but the *larger* archetypal energy it symbolizes. A card's energy is its meaning but with an added sense of movement and change.

A reading you do for yourself is a snapshot of your personal energy configuration at the time of the reading. The cards you pick are the energies that best reflect your situation at that moment.

Just as a snapshot stops the action of a real scene, a reading freezes the flow of your life. But life goes on after a photo is taken, and so do the energies reflected in a reading. Two readings done one after the other rarely contain the exact same cards. The energy pattern changes, even in that short time.

When you do a reading, the cards you draw represent energies important to you at that precise moment. Each one is at a certain point in its individual cycle. One may be strong, another weak. One may be on the rise, another fading. To understand the reading, you need to know the status of each energy—where it is in its cycle.

The orientation of a card gives you this information. Orientation is the direction a card faces on the reading surface (or as you hold it). A card can be upright (normal view) or reversed (upside down).

Figure I (below) is a picture of how an energy rises and falls over time. There is a horizontal line dividing the energy curve in half. The section above the line covers the period when the energy is strong—at or near its peak. The section below the line covers those periods when the energy is weak—either just beginning (left) or ending (right).

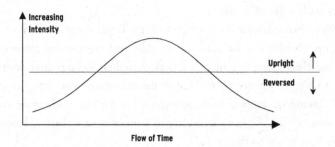

Figure 1. How energy rises and falls over time.

We can now relate card orientation to energy in this way: an upright card represents an energy in the part of its cycle above the line. A reversed card represents an energy in the part of its cycle below the line.

Upright cards stand for energies that are strong and well developed. They have a clear, active presence. You recognize their impact in the situation.

Reversed cards stand for energies that are absent, weak, or undeveloped. They are not clear and obvious. You can't easily recognize their presence for the moment.

For example, an upright World in a reading could imply happiness is strongly present. You feel pleased with life and quite fulfilled. A reversed World would suggest a lower level or unrealized happiness—for now.

An energy does not become its opposite when reversed. A card's essential nature stays the same no matter what its orientation. In our example, a reversed World would not show active unhappiness (the opposite of happiness). It shows the energy of happiness is low—a subtle difference! True unhappiness has its own active energy and might appear in a reading as a card such as the Nine of Swords.

Imagine the energy curve as an island in the ocean. What you can see of the island is its surface above the water—trees, sand, rocks, and so forth. These things are *obvious*. Above the surface is the part of the island we can see; below the surface is the part we can't see. Although this part is hidden, it's still present.

Sometimes a reversed card represents an energy that is hidden, rejected, or ignored. It is not available because it hasn't yet "come to the surface." An upright Devil might show an obsession you acknowledge; a reversed Devil, one you deny. A denied obsession is unconscious but very real.

A reversed energy can also be at a low level because it's new and tentative—in the early part of its cycle, or because it's almost gone—approaching the end of its cycle. In both cases the energy is weak, but for quite different reasons.

CHAPTER 2

Recognizing Energy Phases

The energy cycle is made up of three distinct phases—early, middle, and late—as illustrated in Figure 2.

Each phase has its own unique character:

Early-phase energy is just beginning. It's not yet developed, but it's growing. It's moving toward full expression in the future.

Middle-phase energy is strong and developed. It's clear, immediate, and obvious in the present.

Late-phase energy is on the decline. It's losing power and clarity. The energy's full expression is in the past.

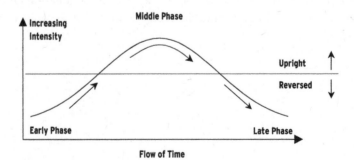

Figure 2. The three distinct phases of the energy cycle: early, middle, and late.

An upright card represents an energy in the strong, middle phase of its cycle (above the line in Figure 2). Interpreting upright cards is fairly straightforward because there's only one possible phase. The energy is well developed, active, and near full strength. In part two, each card description begins with the meaning of the card when upright—the *middle phase* of the card's energy.

A reversed card is not so easy to identify because its weak energy can be in either of two phases: early or late (below the line to the left or right, respectively, in Figure 2). You can tell which phase applies by looking at how the card fits into the overall situation of your question and reading.

The best clue to identifying the energy phase will come from an awareness of timing. A reversed card is in the early phase if you haven't really experienced its energy as yet. It may be new or tied to some upcoming event. A reversed Five of Swords would be in the early phase if you know you're heading into some contest or battle.

A reversed card is late phase if you've already experienced its energy. It has been active in the situation in a way you can easily recognize but is now past. A reversed Five of Swords would be in the late phase if you've gone through some battle that is now winding down.

You can also identify the phase by sensing the "feel" of an energy. Is it growing or fading? A growing energy is developing, expanding, or moving toward you. You sense it's going to get stronger and more noticeable. A fading energy is contracting or moving away. It's getting weaker and less noticeable.

The reversed Knight of Wands can represent a low level of passion. The passion is early phase if you feel it's likely to get stronger and more compelling. The passion is late phase if it has been strong but now has lost most of its drive and power.

Sometimes a reversed card shows an energy that's absent. Its level is so low that, to all intents and purposes, it doesn't exist. But appearances can be deceiving! If a card appears in a reading, you can assume its energy is playing some kind of role. The energy may be so new that you can't perceive it yet. It may only seem absent because you're unconscious of it, but it's still having an impact. In the card description section of part two, I have included meanings for this "absent" energy.

Let's look at how you might interpret one reversed card's energy. I'll use the Five of Pentacles as an example. Some meanings for this card are Hard Times, Ill Health, and Rejection.

If the Five of Pentacles is upright, you know its energy is in the middle phase of its cycle. It's strong and developed. You might be in debt, out of a job, sick, or suffering a rejection. These are all obvious instances of the energy of hard times in the present.

If reversed, the Five of Pentacles energy is either absent, weak, or undeveloped. If no hardship comes to mind, it may indeed be absent for the moment, but you should still be on the alert! You may be about to get sick but don't know it because there are no symptoms. You may think you're unconcerned about money, but an unconscious fear of poverty is affecting you nonetheless.

If you can identify a hardship, but it's not yet strong or active, the energy is in the early phase. Perhaps you've heard rumors of layoffs, but no one has yet been let go. Maybe you've had some minor chest pains, but you've been ignoring them.

If you've already experienced a hardship, the energy is in the late phase. It has passed through your life. If you were laid off, that would be a major difficulty that's now behind you. If you've been having serious money problems, you can guess they're now going to lessen.

Knowing an energy's phase can help you deal with the energy effectively. You can anticipate what to expect, knowing where the energy is in its cycle.

Another aspect of energy cycles is their tendency to repeat. Energies don't begin and end abruptly. They flow in waves. When we finish one breath, we begin another. A love affair ends, but a new one begins. Each instance is unique, but the pattern repeats.

It's helpful to look for repeating energy cycles in your life so you can encourage the positive ones and avoid the negative. The best time to affect a repeating cycle is when the energy is low—in the early or late phase. Once a cycle is in full swing, the energy is strong and hard to change.

Early Phase

An early phase energy is just developing, but you can experience it as either new or repeating.

A new energy has a fresh quality. You respond to it spontaneously. It can be delightful or unnerving, depending on the energy. The past is not dictating your reaction, but you also don't have experience to guide you.

A repeating energy is one you recognize. It has been present in your life before and is now making a repeat appearance. The energy is familiar. It triggers old patterns. Your responses may be more predictable but also more assured. Assumptions from the past may color your experience, but you also have more knowledge to go by.

Sometimes you can experience an energy as if for the first time even though it's familiar. You deliberately decide to let go of the past and greet the energy as new. Let's say you've drawn the Nine of Cups reversed. This card might show a possible sensual encounter in the future. The event may be new or one you've enjoyed before. In either case, it will be more delightful if treated as a first!

Sometimes you might see in a reversed card the beginning of some familiar but unwanted energy coming back into your life—a troublesome pattern you recognize all too well. But since the energy is early phase, you have a wonderful opportunity to change your habitual response. Awareness helps you break the pattern. The Nine of Swords reversed can show a worry beginning to trouble you. If you recognize that worry as an old habit, you can choose to avoid such thoughts if they are not helping.

To figure out if an early-phase energy is repeating, ask yourself the following questions:

- Is this energy familiar?
- Have I been in this situation before?
- Are my reactions predictable?
- Do I feel compelled to act in certain ways?
- Is it hard for me to change my behavior?
- Can others predict my actions?

Late Phase

Late-phase energy is fading, but you can experience it as either complete or incomplete.

A completed energy brings peace and closure. You can let go with little doubt or hesitation. You know the energy has been resolved, so you can put it to rest.

An incomplete energy is likely to be only temporary. The energy is going to return to be resolved. Sometimes an energy fades because it has been neglected or mishandled. Sometimes the timing wasn't right for it to continue. Such energies will likely rise again at a more opportune moment.

A reversed Justice can show the approaching end of a legal matter. If the case hasn't been resolved to your satisfaction, you may feel the need to start the cycle again. Or you can decide to accept the ruling and move on, thus breaking the cycle.

To figure out if a late-phase energy is incomplete and thus likely to repeat, ask yourself the following questions:

- Am I dissatisfied with what has happened?

- Do I feel compelled to hold on?

- Is something keeping me from releasing?

- Am I sorry this energy is fading?

- Was this energy cut off prematurely?

- Will I want to revisit this energy again?

Knowing that energy tends to repeat helps you appreciate the subtle shifts that occur at the reversed-card stages. You can watch for past influences affecting new energies. You can make sure fading energies are resolved satisfactorily.

CHAPTER 3

A Strategy for Interpreting Reversals

You now have all you need to begin working with reversed cards. In this chapter, I'll describe a strategy you can use to deepen your understanding of any card's meaning in a reading. The strategy is broken up into seven steps:

Steps 1–2: Get a sense of a card's basic energy.

Steps 3–5: Consider how the card's orientation impacts that energy.

Steps 6: Relate the card's energy to other cards in the reading.

Step 7: Decide what to do about the energy, if anything.

These are the steps for a single card. You can repeat them for all the cards in a reading. With each pass, your interpretation will shift a little, but gradually you'll build up a solid understanding of all the energies and their relationships.

This method will help you integrate orientation into your tarot practice. I'll present the whole strategy first, then take you through an example.

Step 1: What is the card's energy?

Get a basic idea of the card's energy—its meaning to you at the time of the reading. Use all the techniques of card interpretation at your disposal including traditional meanings, personal reactions, and your response to the card image. So many meanings are possible. As always with the tarot, much depends on your awareness and intuitive responses in the moment.

Step 2: What is the context for this card's energy?

Place the card's energy within a context. For example, consider how the card relates to what is going on in your life. If you asked a question, how does the card reflect that question? Does it help you arrive at some kind of answer? If the card appears in a spread, how does the meaning of the position it falls in impact the energy?

Step 3: What is the card's orientation?

Note whether the card is upright or reversed. This tells you the strength of the card's energy. If upright, the energy is present, developed, obvious, and active. If reversed, the energy is absent, undeveloped, hidden, or inactive. It's possible you may not agree with the energy level shown by a card, but the reading is suggesting to you its actual strength in the moment.

Step 4: What is the energy's phase? (Reversed cards only)

Try to figure out where the reversed card's energy is in its cycle. It could be:

Absent—the energy does not seem present at all

Early Phase—the energy is somewhat present, but you sense it will be stronger in the future

Late Phase—the energy is somewhat present, but it is not as strong as it was in the past

Step 5: Is this energy new or repeating? Is it complete or incomplete? (Reversed cards only)

Assess whether or not you've experienced this energy before. If it's in the early phase, is it brand-new or familiar—part of a repeating pattern you recognize? If it's in the late phase, does it feel complete or incomplete to you? If the energy seems completely absent, become aware that the energy is indeed hovering around, even if not yet obvious in your experience.

Step 6: Is the card's energy part of a group?

Note if the card belongs to any groups, such as suit or type: major arcana, number card, or court card. Does the energy seem linked to certain other cards, and, if so, how is that energy impacted by those connections?

Step 7: What do I want to do about this energy?

Once you have decided upon your best understanding of a card's energy, you can decide what to do about it. You can encourage, discourage, or simply let the energy be. The choice is up to you!

• • •

Example

You decide to do a reading about a problem at work. This week, your manager told you that she wants you to inform her daily about your progress on a certain project. You think this monitoring is a waste of time. You told her you'd rather inform her when necessary, but she still insists on a daily report.

You do a reading to answer the following question: "What do I need to understand about the disagreement I'm having with my boss?"

You draw the reversed Four of Pentacles in a spread position that indicates the "key feature of the situation."

Step 1: What is the card's energy?

Three traditional keyword meanings for the upright Four of Pentacles are possessiveness, control, and blocked change. In the past, this card has often meant control to you. You see the figure as trying to hold down the coins. He seems to be saying, "You're not going anywhere without my permission!" So, you settle on the control meaning for now.

Step 2: What is the context for the card's energy?

The situation consists of all aspects of your interaction with your boss—both internal and external. Your question narrows the focus down to what "you need to know to better understand the disagreement." The position meaning suggests "control" is a *key feature*.

Step 3: What is the card's orientation?

The card is reversed, so you know its energy is relatively weak. It's not fully developed as yet.

Step 4: What is the energy's phase?

You rule out late phase because your manager's request is new. Early phase seems best, but you wonder why the card is reversed? To you, control is a strong and obvious aspect of this situation, and yet the reading suggests that this energy is low. Are you perhaps misreading the request as a control issue? On the other hand, the control energy may get worse in the future.

Step 5: Is this a repeating energy?

You have to acknowledge that this scenario feels very familiar. You know that you tend to get angry and defensive at any hint of control. Are you setting yourself up for another round of charges and counter-charges?

Step 6: Is the card's energy part of a group?

You look at the other pentacles cards and their locations. Is the Four of Pentacles in a special position group? Can you intuitively link this card with any others? How do these connections enhance or downplay the importance of control as reflected in your card's energy?

Step 7: What do I want to do about this energy?

You still feel there's an element of control in this situation, but you're also willing to now consider the possibility that it may be pretty low. You decide to talk to your manager calmly to find out what her goals are. Then, maybe you can work out an arrangement that will work for both of you.

Your review of the Four of Pentacles led to an unexpected insight. You realized that you *may* have introduced the control energy into this matter yourself, perhaps because of past experiences. If control does turn out to be a growing feature of this situation, you now have a deeper awareness of the dynamics involved.

• • •

As you can see, these steps offer one way to discover the meaning of a card's energy. The benefit of a strategy is that it helps you avoid floundering during interpretation. You have a way to approach each card that leaves you with a useful understanding. The disadvantage is that a strategy tempts you to abandon your intuition to rely on a rote system. You don't want your interpretation to become automatic.

This approach is analytical, but only at first. As you practice with it for a time, your interpretations will become more profound and integrated. In the end, you'll have a trustworthy method for tapping into the wisdom of your Inner Guide.

Part Two

REVERSED
CARD
DESCRIPTIONS

These seventy-eight card descriptions are designed to help you interpret reversed cards in your readings. For each card, there is an upright and reversed section.

Upright

This section presents keywords for the cards: words and phrases that capture distinct meanings and together create an impression of the upright energy of the card. For example, the statement and keywords for the Empress contain:

> "It's a time of <u>mothering</u> and nurturing. <u>Abundance</u> is everywhere. <u>Senses</u> are heightened."

Reversed

This section is organized by the keywords present in the upright card and shows how the energy manifests in a reversal. Three to five keywords are expanded upon for each card, with three phases for each keyword: absent, early, and late. Again, short sample statements are used to show how the card's energy might manifest in each phase. The statements for each phase reflect the nature of that phase.

Absent

"Absent" energy is not immediately apparent, but it is present nonetheless, even if only in potential. Statements for absent energy are in the negative:

> "You're not in a relationship."

> "You have no stamina."

"You're denying your destiny."

"There's little justice at the moment."

Early Phase

Early phase energy may develop in the future, so statements for this phase suggest what *may* happen:

"You may start exploring options."

"A delay may develop."

"You may become strong in the future."

Late Phase

Late phase energy references the past. Statements for this phase show decline or events that have already occurred:

"Your power is fading."

"Someone is less obedient now."

"You've gone through a fateful encounter."

When interpreting a reversed card, read over all the statements given. Look for those that trigger the strongest response. Also, allow yourself to move beyond the statements to similar ones that occur to you. You're not limited to what's written. Adopt a mood of waiting to see what pops into your mind. Often the ideal statement for the occasion will come to you spontaneously. If you get stuck, use the interpretation strategy described in chapter 3.

These reversed card descriptions are for quick reference. For a fuller discussion of cards and their meanings, please refer to *The Big Book of Tarot*.

MAJOR ARCANA

The Fool

Upright

It's a time of beginning. New paths and directions are available. Spontaneity is important. You can live in the moment with trust. Your faith is strong. Everything is unfolding as it should. What appears to be folly is not.

Reversed

Keyword: Beginning

Absent: You can't begin right now. A new direction is not available. People are not willing to explore the unknown. It's not the right time to start a journey. You're not able to take that first step.

Early Phase: You may be ready to start. The journey may be about to begin. A new phase may be coming up. You may initiate a novel plan. The unknown may beckon.

Late Phase: The chance to begin is disappearing. The new opportunity is no longer available. The initiative is less likely now. The start date has passed. The unknown is losing its appeal.

Keyword: Spontaneity

Absent: There's little spontaneity right now. People are not feeling carefree. Impulsive behavior is rare. You're not living in the moment. There are few surprises. No one is breaking the routine.

Early Phase: The atmosphere may become freer. You may let go of expectations. It may get easier to act on the spur of the moment. You may start to feel more uninhibited.

Late Phase: The carefree times are ending. You're no longer willing to improvise. Impromptu decisions are less effective now. Someone is becoming less impetuous. The free and natural mood is fading.

Keyword: Faith

Absent: You lack faith right now. You don't trust the flow. It's not easy to feel sure. Your sense of security is not strong. Confidence is low. You don't have much hope.

Early Phase: Your faith may return. It may get easier to believe. You may gain more confidence. The situation may start to feel secure. Someone may become more willing to believe.

Late Phase: You're losing faith. Hope is fading. You're not as confident as you were. Someone is no longer trusting. The time of innocence is past.

Keyword: Apparent Folly

Absent: You're not willing to take a "crazy" chance. You don't trust what your heart is telling you. You're afraid to look foolish. Someone is not supporting your "silly" dream. Outrageous behavior is no longer accepted.

Early Phase: You may start to pursue a dream. You may become involved in some foolishness. You may be ready to take a wild chance. You may decide to go for it, even if you fail.

Late Phase: The time to be wild and crazy has passed. You're more disillusioned now. It's no longer possible to pursue your dream. A bit of foolishness is behind you.

The Magician

Upright

It's a time of action. You can do what needs to be done. Having conscious awareness is important. Your concentration level is high. Total commitment is possible. Power is available. You can make a strong impact.

Reversed

Keyword: Action

Absent: You can't take action right now. You're unable to maneuver. Plans can't be implemented. Your talents are not being used. There's not much happening. The work is not getting done.

Early Phase: The time for action may be approaching. You may be ready to make your move. The plan may be going forward. You may have a chance to do what you have to do. There may be more activity in the future.

Late Phase: The time for action is ending. The activity level is decreasing. There's less support for your exploits now. Someone is using less force. People are no longer carrying out the plan.

Keyword: Conscious Awareness

Absent: You don't know what's going on. Someone is clueless. You're not sure of your motivations. The situation is not clear to you. True intentions are not being expressed.

Early Phase: You may begin to catch on. You may grow more aware. The true nature of the situation may become clear. People may start to speak openly. You may need to stay on top of things in the future.

Late Phase: You're becoming less aware. You're no longer sure what's happening. Your clarity of purpose is disappearing. It's not as easy to defend your position now. Understanding is fading.

Keyword: Concentration

Absent: You can't concentrate. You're not focused. There's no singleness of purpose. It's hard to stay centered. People lack commitment. Someone is off-message.
Early Phase: You may start to concentrate better. It may get easier to stay focused. Your sense of purpose may return. Dedication may grow. You may begin to commit to your goal.
Late Phase: You're no longer able to avoid distractions. Your commitment is not as strong. People are less dedicated now. The period of concentration is ending. Your energies are no longer focused.

Keyword: Power

Absent: You lack power at the moment. Your vitality is low. You're not having the impact you desire. You can't accomplish your goals. Energy is not available. Vigor is lacking.
Early Phase: You may become more powerful. You may start to make your presence known. Strength may increase. Your influence may grow. Potency may return.
Late Phase: Your power is decreasing. You're no longer as vigorous. The ability to sway the group is fading. Someone's prestige is declining. There's less energy available.

The High Priestess

Upright

It's a time of nonaction. Events are unfolding on their own. Unconscious awareness is a factor. Your knowledge runs deep. There is great potential in the situation. Mystery is present. All is not being revealed.

Reversed

Keyword: Nonaction

Absent: You can't be inactive right now. It's not easy to stay calm. Being passive is not an option. You resist having to wait. Someone can't stay uninvolved.

Early Phase: You may begin to withdraw. You may have to lay low for a while. A quiet time may be approaching. You may be idle in the future. Someone may start to show more patience.

Late Phase: The time of nonaction is ending. You can no longer stand by and watch. You're less inclined to remain passive now. The waiting is over. People are no longer willing to be quiet.

Keyword: Unconscious Awareness

Absent: Your intuition is not working. You're not listening to your inner voice. Unconscious material is not available. Dreams are hazy or hard to remember. Deeper realities are inaccessible.

Early Phase: You may begin to look within. Someone may open to inner truths. Unconscious material may start to surface. You may become aware of different realities.

Late Phase: You're no longer exploring the unconscious. Doors to the inner realms are closing. People are less willing to face hidden truths. It's getting harder to hear your inner voice. Interest in other realities is fading.

Keyword: Potential

Absent: You're not aware of the possibilities. You're denying a talent. Someone is not enabling growth. There's little recognition of potential. People are refusing to consider an opportunity.

Early Phase: You may begin to recognize your potential. A talent may develop. People may open to what could be. The possibilities may get clearer.

Late Phase: Your potential is no longer being recognized. The latent possibilities were not realized. People are less open to growth now. A talent is fading. An opportunity has passed.

Keyword: Mystery

Absent: You're avoiding a mystery. What's hidden is not being revealed. No one is looking past the obvious. There's little interest in the unknown. Someone is covering up a secret.

Early Phase: A mystery may come to light. You may start to look at what's been concealed. You may approach a closed-off area. Someone may be on the point of remembering. The unknown may beckon.

Late Phase: You're moving away from the mystery. The secret has been revealed or covered up. Someone has opened up a can of worms. Interest in the unknown is fading. The shadow-side is less exposed.

The Empress

Upright

It's a time of mothering and nurturing. Abundance is everywhere. There is more than enough for all. Senses are heightened. It's possible to give and receive pleasure. Nature is a vital part of the situation.

Reversed

Keyword: Mothering

Absent: You can't be a mother right now. Giving birth is not possible at the moment. Someone is not nurturing. There's a lack of tenderness. A mother is distant. A child is not connected to someone who cares.

Early Phase: Mothering may become more important. A birth may be approaching. A desire to nurture may grow. You may start to care for someone. A link with a child may come up. A mother may become more involved.

Late Phase: A time of mothering is ending. A birth has past. There is less nurturing now. A mother is not as close. You're becoming separated from a child. The feeling of being cherished is fading.

Keyword: Abundance

Absent: There's a lack of abundance now. Extravagance is not possible. A lavish reward is not in the picture. You can't indulge in luxuries. The path to riches is blocked. Someone feels there is not enough.

Early Phase: You may start to experience more abundance. An ample supply may be forthcoming. You may move toward plenty. There may be more than enough in the future. A surplus may become possible.

Late Phase: The time of profusion is past. People can no longer be extravagant. Wealth is decreasing. There is less to go around now. The coffers are emptying.

Keyword: Senses

Absent: You can't enjoy your senses. Someone is not vibrantly healthy. There's a lack of earthiness. Pleasure is being blocked. One of the senses is not working properly. Physical activity is low. Beauty is not being valued.

Early Phase: You may start feeling more sensual. Pleasure may become more important. Your vigor and energy may return. One of the senses may improve. You may start to focus on your body.

Late Phase: An experience of pleasure is past. You're no longer enjoying your senses. Physical activity is declining. There's less interest in the body now. One of the senses is failing.

Keyword: Nature

Absent: You're not involved with nature right now. Concern for the environment is not strong. Natural ways are not being embraced. You're out of harmony with natural rhythms. There's little connection with Mother Earth.

Early Phase: A relationship with nature may develop. You may start to feel more natural. Environmental protections may increase. Being outdoors may become more important. An experience with nature may occur in the future.

Late Phase: You're no longer involved with animals or plants. A focus on the environment is decreasing. People are feeling less connected with the Earth. There's less support for a natural approach.

The Emperor

Upright

It's a time of fathering. It's important to provide direction. The focus is on structure. A coordinated plan is in place. Authority is an issue. Someone is concerned with control. Regulation and the law are involved.

Reversed

Keyword: Fathering

Absent: You can't be a father right now. Some connection to a father is broken. Someone is not offering security. You're not setting direction for a child. You're not defending someone in your care.

Early Phase: Fathering may become more important. You may begin to provide support. You may develop a connection to a child. A relationship with a father may improve. Someone may start to guide growth.

Late Phase: A time of fathering is ending. You're no longer supporting a child. A father is becoming less involved. The need for protection is decreasing. Being head of the family is no longer an issue.

Keyword: Structure

Absent: There's a lack of structure now. No one is following a plan. Coordination is low. You're not organized. People are not being systematic. Order is being disrupted.

Early Phase: Order may return. A plan may begin to take shape. You may start to coordinate activities. The environment may become more structured. Loose ends may be tied up in the future.

Late Phase: The structure is falling apart. Organization is declining. You're no longer following a plan. The period of order is ending. Fixed relationships are breaking up.

Keyword: Authority

Absent: You don't have authority right now. Someone is not showing leadership. There's a lack of command. Someone is not respected. No one's in charge.

Early Phase: You may start to exert control. An authority figure may become involved. Direction may be imposed. Respect may grow. You may have a chance to become a leader.

Late Phase: You're no longer in authority. You're losing your position of strength. Control is passing to someone else. Leadership is no longer strong. Officials are stepping aside.

Keyword: Regulation

Absent: Rules are not being followed. Standards of behavior are not in place. No one is regulating the system. Law and order are lacking. The regimen is not being followed.

Early Phase: You may begin to establish rules. A legal matter may become important. Contacts with the law may increase. Regulations may be enforced.

Late Phase: A legal matter is being concluded. Rules are decreasing. The monitoring period is over. There's less support for the program now. Regulations are no longer respected.

The Hierophant

Upright

It's a time of education. The pursuit of knowledge is important. Belief systems are having an influence. Traditions are in place. There's a spirit of conformity. Everyone is doing what's expected. A group identity is primary.

Reversed

Keyword: Education

Absent: You can't pursue learning right now. You don't have a chance to study. Someone is not in school. You're having trouble staying informed. Knowledge is hard to come by.

Early Phase: You may begin your studies. Someone may enter school. A thirst for knowledge may grow. You may need more information. A learning session may be about to start.

Late Phase: A time of learning is ending. Your studies are over. Getting an education is no longer a priority. You found out what you needed to know. Understanding is decreasing.

Keyword: Belief Systems

Absent: You lack a belief system. You're rejecting tradition. You don't want to proceed with a ceremony. People are not respecting their heritage. You don't know where to put your faith.

Early Phase: You may be forming a world view. You may be ready to follow a discipline. A ritual may be coming up. You may decide to learn a set of beliefs. Traditions may become more important.

Late Phase: You're losing your beliefs. The traditional ways are no longer appealing. A way of life is disappearing. Your faith has been shaken. The old assumptions are less valid.

Keyword: Conformity

Absent: There's a lack of conformity. No one is following the rules. You can't fit in. Someone won't do what's expected. It's hard to adapt to the system. You're not ready to acquiesce.

Early Phase: You may begin to go along with the program. You may start to be more conventional. People may become more orthodox. Someone may fall in line in the future.

Late Phase: There's less conformity now. People are no longer abiding by the rules. The need to blend in is decreasing. The party line is losing its appeal. Someone is less obedient.

Keyword: Group Identity

Absent: You don't identify with a group. You're not joining an organization. The team is not together. There's little loyalty to the group. Someone is not committed to a communal effort.

Early Phase: You may join a group. You may become part of a team. A spirit of community may be forming. Like-minded people may start coming together. You may decide to add your voice to others.

Late Phase: You're separating from a group. The time of togetherness is ending. Your commitment to the mutual cause is fading. The team is dissolving. There's less commonality.

The Lovers

Upright

It's a time of relationship. You can establish bonds and make connections. Sexuality is important. Passions are strong. Personal beliefs are influential. You can make up your own mind. It's time to consider values and ethical choices.

Reversed

Keyword: Relationship

Absent: You're not in a relationship. A marriage or union is not happening. It's not easy to make a connection. There is little intimacy. Kinship ties are broken. Someone is lacking love. Bonds are weak.

Early Phase: You may begin a relationship. Love may grow. A connection may develop. You may be drawn closer to someone. A marriage or union may occur in the future.

Late Phase: A relationship is ending. There's less intimacy now. You no longer feel love for someone. A family tie is loosening. Communication is decreasing. A partnership is dissolving.

Keyword: Sexuality

Absent: There is little sex right now. Desire is low. You can't express your passion. You're not attracted to someone sexually. Making love is not an option.

Early Phase: You may begin to feel a sexual attraction. Desire may grow. You may become more passionate. Life-force energy may increase. A sexual relationship may be initiated in the future.

Late Phase: There are few opportunities to be sexual now. You're losing your desire. The passionate phase is ending. The atmosphere is no longer sexually charged. The life-force energy is not as strong.

Keyword: Personal Beliefs

Absent: Your personal beliefs are not solid. You can't decide for yourself. It's difficult to know where you stand. Someone is not accepting your opinion. You can't challenge the entrenched system.

Early Phase: You may begin to think for yourself. You may come to your own conclusions. Someone may question the group consensus. A maverick thinker may get involved.

Late Phase: Your personal views are no longer involved. Your belief system has been challenged. The chance to make up your own mind is ending. It's harder to stay true to yourself at this point.

Keyword: Values

Absent: Values are not a high priority right now. You're avoiding an ethical choice. Someone is not staying true to ideals. Standards are not being met. No one is focused on what's right.

Early Phase: You may become more concerned with values. A moral or ethical dilemma may come up. You may have to choose between right and wrong. You may rediscover your ideals.

Late Phase: A code of ethics is no longer in place. Values are being discarded. Integrity is less of an issue now. The moment of temptation has passed. Your struggle with your ideals is ending.

The Chariot

Upright

It's a time of victory. A triumph is in the air. Your will is strong. You can accomplish any goal. There's a need for self-assertion. Someone's interests are at stake. Powerful impulses are involved. Hard control is an issue.

Reversed

Keyword: Victory

Absent: You're not achieving a victory. The win is not happening. Someone is not beating the competition. The goal is not in sight right now. Domination is not possible.

Early Phase: You may begin to be successful. A victory may become possible in the future. You may triumph in the end. The path to the top may begin soon. A mood of conquest may develop.

Late Phase: The victory is behind you. Your string of wins is ending. A moment of triumph is in the past. You're no longer dominating. The battle is winding down.

Keyword: Will

Absent: You lack the determination to succeed. Your will is not strong right now. Self-discipline is low. Someone lacks willpower. The desire is not there. Your resolve is weak.

Early Phase: You may start to get focused. Your determination may grow. The desire for success may become stronger. Someone may show more discipline.

Late Phase: Your concentration is decreasing. You can no longer sustain an effort. The will to achieve is fading. You're less intent now. Your strength of purpose is weakening.

Keyword: Self-Assertion

Absent: You're not asserting yourself. You're not putting yourself forward. People don't know who you are. There's little need to be first. Your actions are not ego based.

Early Phase: You may become more assertive. You may start to stand up for yourself. Self-confidence may grow. You may be ready to ask for what you want.

Late Phase: You're less assertive now. You're no longer making your presence felt. Your desire to be first is decreasing. Selfish needs are losing importance. It's no longer necessary to grab the attention.

Keyword: Hard Control

Absent: There's a lack of hard control. Discipline is not effective. Someone is not maintaining order. Authority is missing. You're not keeping a lid on your feelings. You're not embracing the tough approach.

Early Phase: Strong controls may begin to be implemented. You may need to be firm in the future. Strict measures may become necessary. You may start to master your emotions.

Late Phase: The rigid controls are loosening. You're no longer in control. The reins of power are slipping away. The need to be strict is decreasing. You're putting an oppressive environment behind you.

Strength

Upright

It's a time for strength. You can endure and thrive. Patience is important when dealing with frustration. There is room for compassion and sympathy. Soft control is effective now.

Reversed

Keyword: Strength

Absent: You're not feeling strong. Resolve is low. You have no stamina. There's a lack of toughness. Someone can't be counted on. The power to prevail is low.

Early Phase: You may begin to feel stronger. Energy may return. You may become more determined. The will to survive may grow. Your power may build.

Late Phase: Your strength is declining. You're no longer feeling vigorous. You've lost heart. Energy is draining out of the situation. People are losing resolve. The peak of power is past.

Keyword: Patience

Absent: There's little patience at the moment. You can't keep your temper. There's little self-control. You're having trouble waiting. No one is accepting. Frustration throws you off.

Early Phase: You may become more patient. It may get easier to wait. You may develop calm endurance. You may need to bide your time. People may become more accepting.

Late Phase: You're losing patience. You can't wait any longer. The period of resigned acceptance is over. Suffering in silence is no longer an option. You're losing your composure.

Keyword: Compassion

Absent: There's a lack of compassion. You don't feel sympathetic. Someone is not being kind. Mistakes are not being tolerated. Tender feelings can't be expressed. Pity is lacking.

Early Phase: You may start to feel sympathy. Tolerance may grow. People may show more kindness. A mood of good will may develop. You may begin to feel sorry for someone.

Late Phase: Compassion is fading. You no longer feel kindly disposed. The era of good intentions is ending. Well-meaning gestures are becoming less frequent.

Keyword: Soft Control

Absent: You're not using soft control. Someone refuses to be manipulated. Persuasion is not working. You're not wearing velvet gloves. Attempts to influence are not subtle.

Early Phase: You may start to guide indirectly. You're considering a delicate approach. People may become more accommodating. A lighter touch may be applied in the future.

Late Phase: The period of benevolent control is ending. You're no longer open to influence. Attempts to persuade are decreasing. People are less willing to go along gracefully.

The Hermit

Upright

It's a time of introspection. You can learn much by looking within. Searching for answers is important right now. Guidance can be given and received. There's a need for solitude. Someone is withdrawing from involvement.

Reversed

Keyword: Introspection

Absent: You're not feeling introspective right now. There's little time for inner exploring. Motivations are not an issue. Unconscious material is inaccessible. You can't focus on yourself.

Early Phase: You may start to look within. You may begin to question your identity. You may have more time to think in the future. Quiet time may become important. An inner journey may be approaching.

Late Phase: Your period of soul-searching is past. You're less inclined to focus inward now. You had a significant inner experience. Self-analysis is no longer necessary.

Keyword: Searching

Absent: You're not seeking right now. A personal quest is on hold. Someone is not looking for the truth. The hunt is stalled. No one is pursuing the investigation.

Early Phase: You may begin to look for answers. You may need to learn more. People may initiate a search. A quest may begin. Someone may start looking below the surface.

Late Phase: The search is ending. You're no longer curious to learn more. A period of questioning is behind you. The hunger for truth is fading. The desire to look around is decreasing.

Keyword: Guidance

Absent: There's little guidance. You're not offering or receiving advice. Someone's opinion is not welcome. A mentor or teacher is unavailable. Wisdom is hard to come by.

Early Phase: You may decide to seek guidance. An outside opinion may become useful. An encounter with a teacher or guru may occur in the future. You may begin a therapeutic program.

Late Phase: You're losing a source of guidance. Your counsel is no longer desired. There's less help available now. Someone is rejecting supervision. Suggestions are dwindling.

Keyword: Solitude

Absent: Solitude is not possible. You can't withdraw from the situation. You have little desire to be alone. Someone is not in seclusion now. You can't get away from it all.

Early Phase: You may become more private. A need for solitude may grow. Someone may decide to live alone. You may be more isolated in the future. Quiet time may gain appeal.

Late Phase: Your period of solitude is ending. You're no longer on your own. The feelings of separation are fading. There's less need to be apart now. Someone is leaving a private world.

Wheel of Fortune

Upright

It's a time of destiny. Your fate is greeting you. A turning point has been reached. Which way will you go? There is great movement and change. A personal vision is meaningful to you and others.

Reversed

Keyword: Destiny

Absent: You're denying your destiny. You're not taking advantage of chance. It's hard to accept this special moment. Your fate is not in your hands. Karma is not being resolved.

Early Phase: You may begin to sense the action of fate. A chance encounter may become important. The threads of your life may come together. A surprise twist may be possible in the future.

Late Phase: The moment of destiny has passed. You're no longer open to the fortunes of fate. An unexpected event is behind you. The role of chance is decreasing. The karmic moment has played itself out.

Keyword: Turning Point

Absent: You're not accepting a turning point. You don't want to look at change. Someone is resisting a new possibility. Reversals are not an option. A change in course is stalled for the moment.

Early Phase: A turning point may be coming up. You may be considering a change of direction. A surprising turn of events could occur. The situation may reverse itself in the future.

Late Phase: The turning point is behind you. Change is less likely at this point. You're no longer open to a new direction. Options are narrowing. A course has been set, one way or the other.

Keyword: Movement

Absent: There's little movement now. The activity level is low. You're not getting involved. There's not much happening. New developments are rare. The pace is slow.

Early Phase: The pace may pick up. You may start to notice more activity. People may move around more. The agitation may become more obvious. Everyone may begin to hurry.

Late Phase: There's less activity now. The pace is slowing. You're no longer moving around much. The number of changes is decreasing. There's less switching around.

Keyword: Personal Vision

Absent: You're lacking a personal vision. You're not sure of your role and purpose. You've lost touch with your goals. Nothing seems to make sense. The connections don't add up.

Early Phase: You may become more aware. You may begin to understand yourself. Patterns may start to make sense. Your outlook may expand. An epiphany may occur in the future.

Late Phase: Your personal vision is behind you. You're moving beyond a moment of clarity. Your perspective is no longer all-encompassing. There's less understanding now. You're losing touch with your dream.

Justice

Upright

It's a time of justice. Matters of principle and fair play are important. Responsibility is an issue. People are being held accountable. A decision is being reached. The action of cause and effect is clear.

Reversed

Keyword: Justice

Absent: There's little justice. The fair solution is not on the table. You're not being impartial. People are not committed to what's right. Someone's not getting a fair deal. Legal matters are not being resolved.

Early Phase: You may seek justice. Questions of fairness may come up. Principles may become important. Someone may seek equal treatment. You may get involved with the law.

Late Phase: The time for justice has passed. You're no longer concerned with a legal matter. The focus on equality is decreasing. Principles are being abandoned. Fair play is less of an issue now.

Keyword: Responsibility

Absent: No one is taking responsibility. Someone is not being accountable. You're not willing to take the heat. Old debts are going unsettled. The obligation is not yours. No one is to blame.

Early Phase: You may start to assume responsibility. You may take charge. Someone may admit involvement. People may become more reliable. You may need to answer for your deeds.

Late Phase: The conscientious period is ending. People are less willing to meet obligations. You no longer have to bear the brunt. The finger-pointing is behind you. Someone is not as trustworthy now.

Keyword: Decision

Absent: A decision is not being made. A judgment has not been rendered. No one is coming to a conclusion. The jury is out. You can't make up your mind. Someone is avoiding a choice.

Early Phase: You may be approaching a decision. A need for resolution may develop. You may start to explore options. Someone may need to weigh all sides. The verdict may be on the way.

Late Phase: The period of judgment is past. A choice has been made, or the time for choosing is ending. A verdict was rendered. Someone is less decisive now. Resolution is no longer important.

Keyword: Cause and Effect

Absent: You can't see a cause-and-effect relationship. Reasons aren't clear to you. You don't understanding the connections. The karma of the situation is obscure. Results don't match efforts.

Early Phase: You may begin to see patterns. The impact of the past may become obvious. The situation may start to make sense. You may be causing future effects now.

Late Phase: The cause-and-effect connections are less clear. You no longer understand why. A fateful result has occurred, and you don't recognize the cause.

The Hanged Man

Upright

It's a time of letting go. You can surrender to your experience. A reversal is possible. The situation may change completely. A feeling of suspension exists. Action and time are on hold. A sacrifice is in the air.

Reversed

Keyword: Letting Go

Absent: You're having trouble letting go. Emotions are not being released. Someone is resisting. The struggle is not over. You can't accept what is.

Early Phase: You may begin to relinquish control. You may become more vulnerable. You may need to surrender in the future. Someone may be getting ready to yield. You may have to renounce a claim.

Late Phase: The time for letting go is over. The release is behind you now. Someone or something was set free. The mood is less open now. The moment for capitulation has passed.

Keyword: Reversal

Absent: A reversal is not happening. You're not changing your mind. The old order is not being replaced. Someone is not doing an about-face. You're not switching to the opposite.

Early Phase: A change of direction may be approaching. You may switch. Someone may be going to flip. You may need to turn the situation around. A ruling may be overturned.

Late Phase: The moment for reversal is behind you. The situation is less likely to change now. You're no longer thinking of switching. The urge to revoke or recant is decreasing.

Keyword: Suspension

Absent: Actions are not being held up. You're not being left hanging. There's little pause in activity. People are not waiting for the best moment. No one is suspended. You're not living in the moment.

Early Phase: You may begin to feel cut off. An interruption may be approaching. An event may be put on hold. The chance of delay may grow. Activity may cease in the future.

Late Phase: The period of suspension is past. You're no longer on hold. The feeling of timelessness is fading. There's less chance for a pause now. The break is ending.

Keyword: Sacrifice

Absent: No sacrifice is occurring. You're not giving up a claim. Someone is not being a martyr. A concession is not being offered. Something is not being relinquished.

Early Phase: You may make a sacrifice. You may consider putting someone else's needs first. You may start to devote yourself to a cause. The need to do without may increase.

Late Phase: A time of sacrifice is behind you. You no longer need to deny yourself. There's less call for selfless service now. The need to do without is decreasing. The mood of martyrdom is fading.

Death

Upright

It's a time of ending. Something is finishing. A transition is in progress. You're moving from one state to another. Elimination is important. It's possible to get rid of excess. Inexorable forces are having a strong impact.

Reversed

Keyword: Ending

Absent: An ending is not occurring. You're not completing a task. Goodbyes are not being said. A door is not closing. The last act is not over. Nothing is final yet.

Early Phase: You may be approaching an ending. A parting of the ways may be coming up. You may be entering the end game. A task may be nearing completion. Someone may decide to call it a day.

Late Phase: The time of ending is past. The completion is behind you. Unfinished business is no longer an issue. The old ways are fading. The urge to terminate is decreasing.

Keyword: Transition

Absent: A transition is not in progress. You're not changing status. A transformation is not occurring. A shift is not taking place. You're not being cast adrift.

Early Phase: You may enter a period of transition. A change of condition may be on the horizon. The tide may begin to shift. Someone may be nearing an in-between state. A major transformation may become possible.

Late Phase: A transition is behind you. You're no longer moving from one state to another. A passage is almost completed. People are less interested in change now. The need for conversion is decreasing.

Keyword: Elimination

Absent: Nothing is being eliminated. You're not getting rid of excess. No one is being cast out. A removal is not happening. You can't focus on basics. Unwanted attitudes are not being purged.

Early Phase: You may start to get rid of baggage. Something may be jettisoned in the future. Nonessentials may be on the way out. A dismissal may be in the works. You may begin to simplify.

Late Phase: The period of elimination is behind you. A paring down is less likely now. You're no longer concerned about a removal. The cut has been made. The need to do away with is fading.

Keyword: Inexorable Forces

Absent: The situation is not set in stone. Your fate is not sealed. You don't have to give up. Sweeping changes are not in effect. Dramatic results are not happening. The power of the moment is blocked.

Early Phase: An irresistible event may be on the horizon. An earth-shaking experience may be coming up. Powerful happenings may be building strength. You may get drawn into an inescapable scenario.

Late Phase: A powerful moment is behind you. You've gone through a fateful encounter. A larger-than-life experience has passed. You're no longer at the mercy of forces. The situation is less unyielding now.

Temperance

Upright

It's a time of temperance and moderation. The middle ground holds opportunity. Balance is important. All factors are in equilibrium. Good health is evident. Finding the right combination is possible.

Reversed

Keyword: Temperance

Absent: There's a lack of temperance. You're not being moderate. Someone is not maintaining self-control. You're having trouble showing restraint. Sobriety is not being embraced.

Early Phase: You may start to be more moderate. You may abstain. Someone may look for the middle ground. A centrist position may gain momentum. Forbearance may increase.

Late Phase: The period of moderation is ending. There's less restraint now. You're no longer feeling temperate. The urge to be low key is fading. Discretion is disappearing.

Keyword: Balance

Absent: There's a lack of balance. All positions are not equal. Parity is not being maintained. Parts aren't symmetrical. Harmony is missing. You're not feeling calm and steady. Your composure is shaken.

Early Phase: The situation may grow more balanced. Equilibrium may become a goal. You may start to feel more composed. A focus on equality may begin. You may keep your cool in the future.

Late Phase: The period of balance is ending. Sides are no longer equal. There's less harmony now. A stable situation is breaking up. You're losing composure.

Keyword: Health

Absent: Good health is lacking. Your physical condition is poor. Energy is low. Someone does not feel vigorous and strong. You lack a sense of well-being. Recovery is slow.

Early Phase: Vitality may return. A recovery may begin. You may start to concentrate on your health. More energy may become available. Physical conditioning may improve.

Late Phase: Health is declining. You're feeling less vigorous. The energetic phase is ending. Someone is no longer well. The period of comfort and ease is passing.

Keyword: Combination

Absent: Forces are not being combined. People are not joining together. You're not pooling your resources. The right mix is not in place. Synthesis is lacking.

Early Phase: A merger may occur in the future. A union may become possible. You may start to blend in. An alliance may form. Elements may come together.

Late Phase: An association is breaking up. Parties are no longer joined. There's less consolidation now. The mixture is dissolving. Bonds are not as strong.

The Devil

Upright

It's a time of bondage and obsession. The pull of materialism is strong. Ignorance of the truth is causing concern. Facts are hidden or obscured. There is a mood of hopelessness. The future seems dark and uncertain.

Reversed

Keyword: Bondage

Absent: You're not tied down. An addiction is not controlling. Someone is not willing to submit. You're resisting an obsession. There is no loss of freedom. You're denying a compulsion.

Early Phase: You may begin to feel controlled. An obsession may form. Someone may get hooked. The walls may start to close in. You may be heading into a limiting situation.

Late Phase: The period of bondage is ending. You're putting an obsession behind you. An addiction is less powerful now. You no longer need to submit. A fixation is decreasing.

Keyword: Materialism

Absent: There's a lack of materialism. You're not focused on the physical. The urge to spend is being resisted. Someone is not interested in possessions. Luxury is not important.

Early Phase: You may begin to focus on the material. Acquiring may become important. A desire for physical pleasure may grow. You may start to wish for more comfortable surroundings.

Late Phase: You're losing interest in material possessions. Your desire to spend is decreasing. Surface appearances are less important now. You're no longer focused on the senses.

Keyword: Ignorance

Absent: Ignorance is not a problem. You're not in the dark. Appearances are not deceiving. Being oblivious is not an option. Someone is not blind to the truth.

Early Phase: You may become uninformed. The truth may start to be obscured. You may become out of touch. Someone may begin to look the other way.

Late Phase: The time of not knowing is over. You're no longer ignorant of the truth. Being unenlightened is less desirable now. Your lack of awareness is ending.

Keyword: Hopelessness

Absent: There's no lack of faith. You're not despairing. No one is giving up. You're resisting negativity. The worst scenario is not acceptable. All is not lost.

Early Phase: You may begin to lose hope. Doubts may grow. The future may seem less promising. Your faith may be challenged. A mood of pessimism may develop.

Late Phase: A hopeless period is behind you. Feelings of despair are fading. The world seems less hostile now. You're no longer consumed by doubt. The atmosphere of gloom is lifting.

The Tower

Upright

It's a time of sudden change. Plans are being disrupted. There's a strong release of emotion and energy. A downfall is in progress. Someone's fortunes are being upset. A revelation is occurring. All is being exposed.

Reversed

Keyword: Sudden Change

Absent: Sudden changes are not happening. There's no crisis at the moment. Routines are not being disrupted. You're resisting chaos. There are no surprises.

Early Phase: A crisis may be developing. A major shakeup may be coming. A revolution may be in the works. You may experience a disruption. A drastic change may occur in the future.

Late Phase: The crisis is behind you. The period of upheaval is ending. You're no longer caught in chaos. There's less chance of a surprise now. The disruption is diminishing.

Keyword: Release

Absent: A release is not occurring. You're not letting your feelings out. An explosion is being contained. Energy is not getting discharged. An emotional outburst is not happening.

Early Phase: Anger may be building. You may be ready to explode. You may need to let it all out. The dam may break in the future. A release of energy may become necessary.

Late Phase: The release is behind you. An emotional explosion occurred. You no longer want to lash out. Loss of control is less likely now. The anger is decreasing.

Keyword: Downfall

Absent: A downfall is not occurring. A crash is not in effect. Fortunes aren't lost. Someone is not being humbled. You're resisting a blow to the ego.

Early Phase: A downfall may be in the works. A humbling experience may occur in the future. Someone may topple from the heights. You may be heading toward a collapse.

Late Phase: The downfall is behind you. A period of ruin is over. The breakdown is in the past. You're no longer concerned about failing. The plunge has already occurred.

Keyword: Revelation

Absent: There's no revelation. You don't realize the whole truth. The flash of insight is not occurring. Someone is not seeing past illusions. Answers are not forthcoming.

Early Phase: You may be heading toward a revelation. The truth may be revealed. You may be able to see everything in a flash. An eye-opener may be on the horizon.

Late Phase: A surprise disclosure has occurred. The truth has been divulged. You experienced a burst of awareness. A revelation is behind you. Someone is no longer exposing the truth.

The Star

Upright

It's a time of hope and faith. The situation is full of promise. Inspiration is in the air. Creative answers are possible. A spirit of generosity is important. Giving freely makes a difference. Serenity is possible within and without.

Reversed

Keyword: Hope

Absent: There's a lack of hope. You don't believe in the future. Someone is not thinking positively. Faith is not strong. You can't see the silver lining.

Early Phase: Hope may grow. You may start to feel more confident in the future. The chance for success may improve. Expectations may rise.

Late Phase: Hope is fading. You no longer have faith in a positive outcome. The light at the end of the tunnel is disappearing. Belief is not as strong now. Your spirits are sinking.

Keyword: Inspiration

Absent: Inspiration is missing. You're not getting the answer. Motivation is not strong. A flash of insight is eluding you. Creativity is stalled. You lack someone to encourage you.

Early Phase: You may begin to get inspired. The creative impulse may grow. Someone may become motivated. A positive example may spur you on. You may be stimulated to a higher level.

Late Phase: The period of inspiration is fading. You're less motivated now. The way is no longer clear. The call to greatness is fading. Encouragement is harder to come by.

Keyword: Generosity

Absent: You're not giving gladly. Your heart is not open. Love cannot flow freely. Someone can't extend an offer. A gift is not free of strings. Wealth is not being shared.

Early Phase: You may start to feel generous. A gift may be on the horizon. A spirit of sharing may develop. Someone may extend love and forgiveness. You may contribute openly in the future.

Late Phase: A time of generosity is ending. You're no longer willing or able to offer support. Your heart is not as open now. The charitable impulse is fading. There's less desire to spare no expense.

Keyword: Serenity

Absent: Serenity is lacking. You don't have peace of mind. The situation is not harmonious. It's not easy to relax. You can't maintain your cool.

Early Phase: The environment may become peaceful. You may start to feel calmer. Tranquility may be restored. A period of serenity may be approaching.

Late Phase: You're no longer feeling calm. The mood of serenity is fading. You're losing your ability to stay centered. People are less in harmony now. The moment of peace is behind you.

The Moon

Upright

It's a time of fear and uncertainty. Feelings of anxiety are strong. Someone is caught in an illusion. A fantasy seems real. The world of imagination is key. Events are strange and unusual. Bewilderment is a problem.

Reversed

Keyword: Fear

Absent: You're not afraid right now. A phobia is not strong. Someone is resisting a fear. Feelings of dread are not obvious. The shadow self cannot surface.

Early Phase: You may start to feel anxious. A mood of uncertainty may develop. Someone may become apprehensive. A hidden fear may surface. You may begin to feel some qualms.

Late Phase: Fears are diminishing. An inner demon is less powerful now. You're no longer intimidated. The anxious moments are behind you. The mood of foreboding is disappearing.

Keyword: Illusion

Absent: There's no illusion. You're not under a false impression. The truth is not being distorted. People aren't deceiving themselves. An attempt to mislead is not working. You're not chasing a fantasy.

Early Phase: You may get drawn into an illusion. A false picture may develop. You may start to deceive yourself. The truth may become elusive. Hallucinations may get stronger.

Late Phase: An illusion has been revealed. Appearances are no longer deceiving. The false reality is losing its hold. You're less susceptible to fantasy. Someone has stopped trying to fool you.

Keyword: Imagination

Absent: There's a lack of imagination. People aren't open to the unusual. You can't remember your dreams. Visions are elusive. The unconscious is not available. You're not prone to fantasy right now.

Early Phase: You may begin to use your imagination. You may open to what is strange and bizarre. Unconscious material may surface. Someone may start to indulge in make-believe.

Late Phase: A fantasy is no longer strong. You're less imaginative now. Someone is losing interest in dreams. Fanciful notions are decreasing. The strange happenings are decreasing.

Keyword: Bewilderment

Absent: You're not feeling confused. You haven't lost direction and purpose. Someone is not easily distracted. Circumstances are not puzzling. You have no trouble thinking clearly.

Early Phase: You may start to get disoriented. Uncertainty may grow. The way may become unclear. Someone may begin to get lost. You may lose your bearings.

Late Phase: The period of bewilderment is behind you. You're no longer confused. The aimless wandering is over. The mental fog is lifting. Someone is less disoriented now.

The Sun

Upright

It's a time of enlightenment. New levels of understanding are being realized. Greatness is yours. You are shining forth brilliantly. Health and vitality are strong. You have the assurance you need for success.

Reversed

Keyword: Enlightenment

Absent: You're not realizing the truth. You're not feeling enlightened. There's a lack of understanding. You can't make sense of the situation. The pieces don't fit together.

Early Phase: You may begin to understand. Insights may start to come. You may get closer to a breakthrough. Someone may have an epiphany. An expanded vision may become possible.

Late Phase: The moment of enlightenment is behind you. You experienced an epiphany. There's less awareness now. You're losing your grasp of the truth. The sun is going behind a cloud.

Keyword: Greatness

Absent: Greatness is elusive. You can't achieve your goal. A moment of glory is not happening. Someone is not the center of attention. No one is outstanding right now.

Early Phase: You may start to be noticed. Your light may get brighter. Your talent may develop. A glorious moment may be approaching. Someone may show great promise.

Late Phase: A period of renown is ending. You're no longer standing out. The height of success is behind you. Fame is slipping away. Your time as leader is winding down.

Keyword: Vitality

Absent: There's a lack of vitality. Your strength is low. A vital spark is missing. Someone is not vigorous. You don't feel a zest for life. The atmosphere is not energized.

Early Phase: You may begin to feel animated. The mood may pick up. Your vigor may return. Enthusiasm may grow. People may start to get charged.

Late Phase: Your vitality is decreasing. You no longer have much energy. The life force is diminishing. The dynamic period is behind you. There's less zip in your step now.

Keyword: Assurance

Absent: You're not feeling confident. Assurance is low. Someone can't make a guarantee. There's a lack of certainty. You're afraid to show what you can do.

Early Phase: You may gain some assurance. You may start to trust your abilities. Confidence may return. You may become free and expansive.

Late Phase: You're less confident now. You're no longer certain. People are losing their nerve. Your faith in yourself is fading. Convictions are not as strong now.

Judgement

Upright

It's a time of judgment. A tough decision is being weighed. A moment of rebirth is at hand. A fresh start is happening. You sense an inner calling. You know what you must do. Absolution is possible. Forgiveness is in the air.

Reversed

Keyword: Judgment

Absent: You can't pass judgment. You're not being judged. A decision is not being made. A ruling is not available. No one is making an assessment. Someone is not able to take a stand.

Early Phase: You may have to judge. You may be preparing to make a choice. An opinion may be rendered. Someone may get off the fence. A conclusion may be reached.

Late Phase: There's less judging now. Your actions are no longer under scrutiny. A decision has been made. A day of reckoning is behind you. The period of criticism is ending.

Keyword: Rebirth

Absent: You're not feeling reborn. A transformation is not happening. Someone is not opening to possibilities. A fresh start is failing. Hope is not being renewed.

Early Phase: Someone may start over. A renewal may be in progress. A time of awakening may be coming. You may see everything differently in the future.

Late Phase: The fresh start is ending. A transforming experience is behind you. The bright new beginning is past. Your newfound hope is fading. You're less joyful now.

Keyword: Inner Calling

Absent: You're not aware of your calling. You can't decide on a vocation. You're not sure what you want to do. There's a lack of conviction. Someone is afraid to make a difference.

Early Phase: You may begin to see your path. You may become drawn in a new direction. Self-confidence may be growing. The way forward may get clearer.

Late Phase: You're losing your sense of purpose. You no longer feel committed to a chosen field. Your certainty is draining away. Someone has failed to heed a call.

Keyword: Absolution

Absent: You're not being absolved of guilt. Someone is unable to atone. You're reluctant to ask for forgiveness. You can't release your regrets. Your remorse is not believed.

Early Phase: You may start to seek forgiveness. You may begin to unburden yourself. It may become possible to wipe the slate clean. Someone may be getting ready to atone.

Late Phase: You have experienced absolution. Your guilt has been washed away. The desire to atone is fading. A reprieve is less likely now. Someone is no longer willing to overlook an offense.

The World

Upright

It's a time of integration. All aspects are coming together. Your accomplishment is being recognized. Dreams are coming true. Involvement is important. You feel fully engaged. There's a sense of fulfillment.

Reversed

Keyword: Integration

Absent: There's a lack of integration. People are not joining together. No one is working in unison. You're not feeling whole. There's no connection. Dynamic balance is missing.

Early Phase: You may begin to feel whole. Everything may start coming together. A spirit of unity may develop. A synthesis may become possible. You may be approaching a time of togetherness.

Late Phase: A combination is coming apart. People are no longer united. You're losing your sense of completeness. The parts are separating. There's less coordination now.

Keyword: Accomplishment

Absent: Little is being accomplished. You can't realize your goals. The path to achievement is blocked. There's a lack of productivity. A dream is not manifesting. Prosperity is elusive.

Early Phase: You may be moving toward your goals. Achievements may become possible. A dream may start to be realized. You may start taking your first steps toward success. Prosperity may be returning.

Late Phase: An accomplishment is behind you. A period of achievement is over. You're no longer meeting your goals. The chance to realize your dream is fading. The era of prosperity is ending.

Keyword: Involvement

Absent: There's a lack of involvement. Few people are taking part. You're not feeling engaged. The buy-in is not strong. A gift or talent is not being used. Someone is not wholly committed.

Early Phase: You may begin to get involved. Someone may join the effort. You may be ready to contribute. A desire to serve may grow. Connections may be forged in the future.

Late Phase: There's less involvement now. You're no longer feeling engaged. Someone is pulling away. A period of intense activity is ending. The focus on serving is decreasing.

Keyword: Fulfillment

Absent: You're not feeling fulfilled. There's a lack of contentment. You can't savor the present. Someone is dissatisfied. The moment is not complete. You can't enjoy life. Joy is rare.

Early Phase: You may become more contented. Moments of happiness may start to happen. A feeling of satisfaction may grow. A time of fulfillment may be approaching.

Late Phase: There's less satisfaction now. You're not as content as you were. The mood of happiness is fading. You no longer have peace of mind.

MINOR ARCANA

Ace of Wands

Upright

Wands' fire energy is at your disposal right now. There's an opportunity to use creative force. You can expand your experience of enthusiasm, confidence, and courage.

Reversed

Keyword: Creative Force

Absent: The opportunity to use creative force is missing. You lack an outlet for your abilities. Your talents can't unfold. Nothing new is being proposed. No one is offering a different approach.

Early Phase: You may have a chance to be creative. An original idea may materialize. Someone may come up with a novel approach. A venue for your talent may open up.

Late Phase: The opportunity to use creative force is fading. The chance to do something new is past. The support for original ideas is disappearing. Creative moments are less frequent.

Keyword: Enthusiasm

Absent: The opportunity to be enthusiastic is missing. No one wants to make an effort. You can't contribute actively. The desire is not there. People can't generate any excitement.

Early Phase: You may have a chance to be enthusiastic. An inspiring occasion may occur. Someone may present an exciting proposal. You may back a winner. Support may start building.

Late Phase: The opportunity to be enthusiastic is fading. You're less eager to take part. The ride seems to be over. You're no longer up for the challenge. There are fewer reasons to be optimistic now.

Keyword: Confidence

Absent: The opportunity to show confidence is missing. You can't prove what you can do. No one believes in you. The environment isn't encouraging. You're having trouble convincing others.

Early Phase: You may have a chance to show confidence. An opportunity to prove yourself may be on the way. A test of your skills may be coming up. Your belief in yourself may be put on the line.

Late Phase: The opportunity to show confidence is fading. The moment to convince someone has passed. You can't demonstrate your certainty now. People are no longer focused on your performance.

Keyword: Courage

Absent: The opportunity to show courage is missing. Your bravery is not being tested. You can't face your fear. There are no challenges right now. You can't push past your limits.

Early Phase: You may have a chance to show courage. You may have to face a challenge. A time of testing may be approaching. You may be asked to take a stand.

Late Phase: The opportunity to show courage is fading. You're no longer being challenged. The test of your mettle is past. The fearful situation is ending.

Two of Wands

Upright

It's a time of personal power. You have influence and authority. Others are following your lead. Boldness is the order of the day. It's possible to take risks. Someone's approach shows originality.

Reversed

Keyword: Personal Power

Absent: You lack personal power at the moment. You have little influence. Others are not accepting your authority. You're not asking for the respect that is due. You can't call the shots right now.

Early Phase: You may gain more power. Others may start paying attention to you. Your position may get stronger. You may be able to seize control. You may be put in charge in the future.

Late Phase: Your power is fading. It's no longer as easy to assert authority. People are not paying as much attention to you. The reins are slipping out of your hands.

Keyword: Boldness

Absent: You're not being bold. It's not possible to confront the situation head-on. Someone is failing to take the initiative. No one is speaking out. You're not comfortable gambling or taking risks.

Early Phase: You may become bold. You may need to take a risk. Daring gestures may become necessary. You may have to seize the initiative. A chance to make your move may open up.

Late Phase: You're feeling less daring. Your courage is slipping. The chance to take a risk has passed. You're pulling back from a dangerous situation. The urge to gamble is fading.

Keyword: Originality

Absent: There's a lack of originality. Nothing new is going on. You don't have a chance to do your own thing. No one is taking a novel approach. People are not ready to accept a pioneer.

Early Phase: You may become more creative. It may get easier to diverge from the crowd. A novel path may open up. You may have a unique experience. Something new may occur.

Late Phase: You're feeling less creative. There are fewer novel approaches now. It's no longer easy to adopt your own style. You had a unique experience that is now ending.

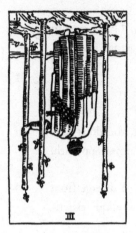

Three of Wands

Upright

It's a time of exploration. You're seeking adventures and new experiences. Foresight is important. It's possible to plan for the future. Questions of leadership are a factor. Someone can provide needed direction.

Reversed

Keyword: Exploration

Absent: There's little exploring going on. People are not open to adventure. You'd rather not deal with unknowns right now. No one is pushing the envelope at the moment.

Early Phase: You may explore new possibilities. An adventure may begin. The future may be more open. You may move into unfamiliar territory. Someone may decide to test uncharted waters.

Late Phase: A period of adventure is ending. The desire to explore is fading. You're no longer interested in dealing with unknowns. There's less need to seek novelty now.

Keyword: Foresight

Absent: There's a lack of foresight. No one is looking at the long-term implications. Grand visions are not being well received. People are not paying attention to the future.

Early Phase: You may need to plan for the future. People may begin taking the long view. It may be possible to foresee problems. You may get premonitions of what's to come.

Late Phase: Attempts to plan for the future are fading. You're no longer showing foresight. There's less focus on looking ahead. People are less interested in the big picture.

Keyword: Leadership

Absent: There's no leadership. Someone has stopped providing direction. You're not in a position to assume control. You can't get a group's support. You're reluctant to show the way.

Early Phase: You may be moving into a leadership position. A chance to take command may open up. You may need to set an example. The main role may fall to you. You may be chosen as a representative.

Late Phase: The opportunity to take command is fading. Your leadership role is behind you. You're no longer setting an example. There's less direction than before. A commander is stepping down.

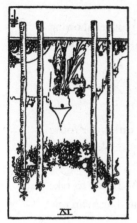

Four of Wands

Upright

It's a time of celebration. People are rejoicing over a happy event or success. You're recognizing a milestone. Freedom is important. It's possible to break free of limitations. Excitement is in the air.

Reversed

Keyword: Celebration

Absent: There's little celebration going on. The ceremony is not going forward. The party is off. Achievements are not being recognized. No one is prepared to claim success.

Early Phase: A major celebration may be approaching. You may experience a joyous occasion. A milestone may be reached. You may receive some congratulations.

Late Phase: The event or ceremony is behind you. The festivities are ending. A milestone was reached and passed. The mood of rejoicing is fading. You no longer have much reason to celebrate.

Keyword: Freedom

Absent: There's a lack of freedom right now. You can't loose the ties that bind. The time's not right for escape. Someone can't accept your independence. No one is being released.

Early Phase: You may decide to claim your freedom. You may let go of inhibitions. You may need to plan an escape. You may cut some cords. Delivery may be at hand.

Late Phase: The break for freedom is behind you. You made your escape. The
cords have been cut. You no longer need to assert your independence.
A period of unlimited possibility is ending.

Keyword: Excitement

Absent: There's little excitement. Not much is going on. Adventure is not a high
priority at the moment. People lack enthusiasm. No surprises are
happening.
Early Phase: You may start looking for excitement. You may begin seeking
thrills. A big adventure may be approaching. Enthusiasm may grow. A
surprise may occur.
Late Phase: The mood of excitement is fading. You're not as enthusiastic as you
were. Thrills are not as important now. The spirit of adventure is not
as strong. The commotion is dying down.

Five of Wands

Upright

It's a time of disagreement and petty quarrels. Everyone is at cross-purposes. Competition is a factor. You have a rival or opponent. Hassles are a problem. You are experiencing minor setbacks.

Reversed

Keyword: Disagreement

Absent: There's little disagreement. Quarrels are nonexistent. People are not picking fights. Debate is being squelched. You're not allowed to question the situation.

Early Phase: You may begin to disagree. Arguments may break out. The lack of consensus may become obvious. People may start quibbling over details.

Late Phase: Disagreements are decreasing. People are no longer arguing much. The period of contention is ending. Differences are not as obvious now. The debate is coming to a close.

Keyword: Competition

Absent: There's little competition. No one's challenging you at the moment. The contest is not in progress. People are not pitted against each other. The match or tournament is not happening.

Early Phase: Competitive elements may increase. A rivalry may develop. You may have a run-in with an opponent. A match may be coming up. A challenge may occur in the future.

Late Phase: The competition is ending. There's less opposition now. You no longer have to deal with a rival or challenger. The match is behind you. People are not as concerned with outdoing each other.

Keyword: Hassles

Absent: You're not experiencing hassles. Petty distractions are not a problem. You're not concerned with trivial details. No roadblocks are in sight.

Early Phase: You may experience a few setbacks. Minor irritations may increase. Some hassles may develop in the future. You may have to deal with some annoying problems.

Late Phase: The hassles are decreasing. You've worked through the worst problems. Resistance is no longer slowing you down. The demands are not as bothersome now.

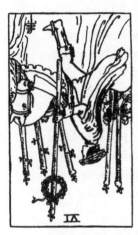

Six of Wands

Upright

It's a time of triumph and success. Victory is in the air. You are enjoying acclaim and well-deserved recognition. Pride is an issue. Self-esteem is turning into arrogance.

Reversed

Keyword: Triumph

Absent: Victory is not happening. Success is not forthcoming. You're not winning right now. Someone is not prevailing. There's little vindication.

Early Phase: You may see signs of success. Victory may be getting closer. Your day of vindication may be approaching. Someone may start winning.

Late Phase: The victory is behind you. The time for success has passed. People are losing their concern with the contest. Chances for vindication are decreasing. You're no longer focused on winning.

Keyword: Acclaim

Absent: Your work is not being acknowledged. There's no applause right now. The award or prize is not being offered. You can't seem to get noticed. Someone is out of the limelight.

Early Phase: You may receive an award or acknowledgement. Hard work may begin to pay off. Your efforts may be recognized. Fame may become important. People may start taking notice.

Late Phase: Praise and acclaim are fading. Your efforts are no longer being recognized. The prize or reward is behind you. Someone received a compliment or pat on the back.

Keyword: Pride

Absent: There's little pride now. People are not confident. Self-esteem is low. Someone is hiding arrogance. You don't have a high opinion of yourself.

Early Phase: You may become more confident. Arrogance may become a problem. Someone may be condescending. Healthy pride may change to overconfidence.

Late Phase: Your pride has taken a blow. You went through a humbling experience. You're feeling less confident. There's less arrogance now. People are no longer sure of themselves.

Seven of Wands

Upright

It's a time of aggression. The advantage is yours if you act forcefully. Defiance is in the air. Someone is refusing to yield. There's a mood of conviction. You are standing up for what you believe.

Reversed

Keyword: Aggression

Absent: There are no hostilities right now. No one is acting aggressively. The time is not right to take what you want. You can't assert yourself. People are not going on the offensive.

Early Phase: Aggression may increase. Hostilities may break out. You may be thinking of a fight. A chance to seize the advantage may come up. You may need to make your point forcefully.

Late Phase: The period of aggression is ending. You're no longer involved in a fight. There's less chance to state your case now. The advantage is no longer yours. Someone has already fired the first shot.

Keyword: Defiance

Absent: Resistance seems futile. No one is being defiant. You can't defend yourself at the moment. It's not possible to hold your position. The time is not right to make a challenge.

Early Phase: You may become more defiant. Resistance may increase. You may need to defend your position. Someone may decide to hold out. People may get their back up.

Late Phase: You're no longer resisting. Defiance is decreasing. Opposition is not as strong now. Challengers are backing off. Refusals are no longer a problem.

Keyword: Conviction

Absent: There's a lack of conviction. No one is sure. It's not easy to stay firm. Someone is not showing much character. You're not convinced you're right.

Early Phase: Conviction may grow. You may gain confidence. You may decide to stay the course. Someone may speak out forcefully. Character may become important.

Late Phase: You're becoming less certain. You're no longer convinced you're right. Someone is giving up. Firm resolutions are getting broken. People are losing the courage to speak out.

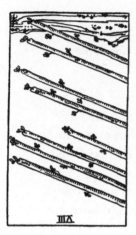

Eight of Wands

Upright

It's a time of quick action. Events are happening rapidly. You can make your move. A conclusion is in progress. Everything is coming together. News is making a difference. The truth is coming out.

Reversed

Keyword: Quick Action

Absent: Little is happening. It's not time for action. Everyone is in low gear. Plans are not being carried out. No one is making a move. Changes are not welcome.

Early Phase: You may declare yourself openly. The pace may pick up. People may decide to act. Changes may become obvious. The time to strike may be coming. Events may start taking off.

Late Phase: The rapid changes are behind you. The pace is slowing. The time for action is past. You no longer have to rush around. You're dealing with the aftermath now.

Keyword: Conclusion

Absent: There's no end in sight. The situation is not getting resolved. No one is taking care of unfinished business. The elements are not coming together. You can't finish. It's difficult to stop.

Early Phase: You may conclude matters. The last act may begin. A final resolution may be approaching. You may be heading toward a culmination.

Late Phase: The situation has been resolved. Everything has been completed. The final act is ending. You're closing out some activity. The last word has nearly been spoken.

Keyword: News

Absent: There's no news at the moment. You lack the information you need. You can't learn more right now. The truth is not coming out. Messages are not getting through.

Early Phase: Some news may be on the way. You may hear an important announcement. You may be getting closer to the truth. Someone may initiate a meaningful conversation.

Late Phase: The news has been delivered. You found out what you needed to know. The truth came out. Less news is getting through. You're no longer in the loop. You have fewer opportunities to be informed.

Nine of Wands

Upright

It's a time of defensiveness. You are preparing for the worst. Extra precautions are in order. Perseverance is important. You can keep going. You have the stamina you need to see the matter through.

Reversed

Keyword: Defensiveness

Absent: There's no need to be defensive now. You're not being attacked. Protections are not in place. Someone is not being careful. People are not assuming the worst.

Early Phase: You may become wary. You may need to defend yourself. Someone may start getting paranoid. The atmosphere may become guarded. Protection may be necessary.

Late Phase: You're no longer defensive. The need to be guarded is ending. There's less chance of an attack now. The mood of paranoia is decreasing. Extra precautions are no longer required.

Keyword: Perseverance

Absent: There's a lack of persistence. You're not committed to the effort. People are not staying the course. Someone is not following through. You don't want to keep trying.

Early Phase: Your resolve may grow. You may get more committed. People may show more determination. You may decide to keep going. Multiple attempts may become necessary.

Late Phase: Commitment is weakening. You're not trying as hard now. Your resolve is fading. You got knocked down and don't want to get up again. The effort no longer seems worth it.

Keyword: Stamina

Absent: You don't have much energy. Your strength is low. It's not possible to keep up the pace. You can't go on because of fatigue. There's a lack of staying power. Reserves are depleted.

Early Phase: Your strength may return. It may get easier to keep up the pace. You may develop more stamina. You may need to hold fast. A test of staying power may be coming up.

Late Phase: Your energy is decreasing. Your strength is wearing out. It's no longer possible to keep going. Your endurance is not what it was. You're letting up a bit. The test of your staying power is ending.

Ten of Wands

Upright

It's a time of overextending. You're trying to do too much. Someone's shouldering most of the work. Burdens are piling up. There are too many responsibilities. You have to struggle. It's an uphill fight.

Reversed

Keyword: Overextending

Absent: You're not overextended. The work load is not excessive. No overtime is required. You don't need to do extra right now. You're not responsible for someone else.

Early Phase: You may become overextended. It may get harder to say "no." The lion's share may fall to you. There may be extra work in the future. You may have to delegate.

Late Phase: Demands are decreasing. You no longer have to shoulder the responsibility. There's less overtime now. You've passed on some of the work.

Keyword: Burdens

Absent: You aren't feeling burdened. There are few duties right now. You're not being blamed. No one is holding you accountable. The load is not too heavy at the moment.

Early Phase: You may start to feel burdened. The work may increase. You may get in over your head. A taxing problem may be looming. Worries may become more oppressive. Accountability may become an issue.

Late Phase: The burdens are decreasing. The unpleasantness is behind you. You've managed to get off the treadmill. You're no longer the main one responsible. The load is lighter now.

Keyword: Struggle

Absent: You don't need to struggle. Resistance is unnecessary. The current is not flowing against you. People are not putting up a fight. The hard way is not the only way.

Early Phase: A struggle may begin. Resistance may develop. You may need to fight for every gain. The path ahead may be steep. The opposition may make your work harder.

Late Phase: The struggle is ending. There's less resistance now. You no longer need to work so hard. The path is heading downhill. The tough times are behind you.

Page of Wands

Upright

Wands' energy is available to help you move in a new direction. The call to be creative, enthusiastic, confident, and courageous is strong right now. Take this chance to go beyond your usual limits and habits!

Reversed

Keywords: Be Creative, Be Enthusiastic, Be Confident, Be Courageous

Absent: The time is NOT right, or you CAN'T follow the call to:

take a novel approach, be original, invent a new way, express yourself freely, get excited, show passion, be the first in line, jump in with both feet, be self-assured, know you can be successful, demonstrate will, be a leader, take a risk, have an adventure, overcome fear, push past doubt.

Early Phase: The time MAY BE APPROACHING when you'll have a chance to:

use your art, show what you can do, come up with a fresh solution, use imagination, get your blood flowing, be eager, feel zest for life, support wholeheartedly, believe in yourself, have faith, accept your convictions, be sure, be assertive, jump without a net, be a hero, show your nerve.

Late Phase: The time is ENDING for any chance to:

show your ingenuity, be resourceful, take a different path, suggest something novel, volunteer, get behind the idea, energize others, join in the action, trust yourself, be certain, set aside doubts, put your best foot forward, make a bold move, stick your neck out, blow the whistle, take the heat.

Knight of Wands

Upright

Wands' energy is extra strong. You, someone else, or the situation may be charming, self-confident, daring, adventurous, and passionate OR superficial, cocky, foolhardy, restless, and hot-tempered.

Reversed

Keywords (Positive): Charming, Self-Confident, Daring, Adventurous, Passionate

Keywords (Negative): Superficial, Cocky, Foolhardy, Restless, Hot-Tempered

Absent: You or someone else is NOT:

> being charming, generating excitement, having complete confidence, taking on the world, risking fearlessly, becoming a hero, seeking change, rising to the challenge, being passionate, taking a vocal stand OR being insensitive, going after sexual conquests, bragging too much, overestimating abilities, taking foolish risks, being a daredevil, requiring constant stimulation, moving around restlessly, being hot-tempered, acting without thinking.

Early Phase: You or another person MAY:

> become physically attractive, be seductive, have a can-do attitude, be self-assured, tackle what others avoid, be bold, look for adventure, make things happen, feel strong loyalties, jump in with both feet OR avoid being serious, say or do what's expedient, show off, be brash, make rash statements, be impetuous, refuse to set down roots, avoid commitment, get hot under the collar, lash out.

Late Phase: You or another person is NO LONGER:

> being glamorous, overly concerned with being attractive, convinced of a talent, being self-reliant, ready and willing to volunteer, being

discrete, daring to act, ready for a challenge, feeling ardent, showing desire OR being thoughtless, focused on the superficial, overly nervy, boasting, endangering self and others, being foolhardy, constantly moving on, too restless, always ready for a fight, looking for trouble.

Queen of Wands

Upright

Wands' energy is present as a state of being. A mood that is attractive, wholehearted, energetic, cheerful, and self-assured is evident. You or someone else is adopting or could adopt the mood of a cheerleader, athlete, champion, group leader, jock, host/hostess, enthusiast, master of ceremonies, or star.

Reversed

Keywords: Attractive, Wholehearted, Energetic, Cheerful, Self-assured

Absent: The mood of you or someone else is NOT:
> warm, outgoing, enthusiastic, wholehearted, lively, vibrant, cheerful, upbeat, poised, unflappable.

Early Phase: The mood of you or someone else MAY BECOME:
> sexy, attractive, dedicated, earnest, vigorous, energetic, sunny, optimistic, self-confident, assured.

Late Phase: The mood of you or someone else is NO LONGER:
> appealing, popular, passionate, vivacious, active, athletic, encouraging, bright, self-possessed, composed.

King of Wands

Upright

Wands' energy is present in an active, outgoing way. Actions that are creative, inspiring, forceful, charismatic, and bold are evident. You or someone else is acting or could act as a leader, director, commander, pioneer, trendsetter, trailblazer, pacesetter, prophet, inventor, or creator.

Reversed

Keywords: Creative, Inspiring, Forceful, Charismatic, Bold

Absent: You or someone else is NOT:
    acting creatively, developing the new, instilling confidence, leading, dominating, commanding respect, attracting attention, wowing others, demonstrating courage, confronting opposition directly.

Early Phase: You or someone else MAY BEGIN to:
    show more originality, take an unusual approach, generate enthusiasm, set an example, act assertively, demand compliance, get noticed, become popular, take more chances, dare to be different.

Late Phase: You or someone else is NO LONGER:
    taking creative chances, going in new directions, showing the way, inspiring, carrying authority well, forcing the issue, acting outrageous, being talked about, ignoring what others think, grabbing the bull by the horns.

Ace of Cups

Upright

Cups' water energy is at your disposal right now. There's an opportunity to use emotional force. You can expand your experience of intuition, intimacy, and love.

Reversed

Keyword: Emotional Force

Absent: The opportunity to use emotional force is missing. You lack an outlet for your feelings. Your heart doesn't lead. The environment doesn't encourage passion. Strong emotions are being denied.

Early Phase: You may have a chance to use emotional force. An opportunity to express your feelings may open up. Someone may respond strongly in the future. An emotional encounter is on the horizon.

Late Phase: The chance to use emotional force is fading. The chance to show your feelings is past. The time for passion is ending. You can no longer respond from the heart.

Keyword: Intuition

Absent: The opportunity to be intuitive is missing. No one respects your hunches. You can't contribute your insights. Inner awareness is not present. You're not trusting your gut reaction.

Early Phase: You may have a chance to be intuitive. Some time to go within may open up. An experience of direct knowing may occur. A psychic occasion may come up.

Late Phase: The opportunity to be intuitive is fading. You're less able to go within now. Experiences of direct knowing are decreasing. Your gut reactions are no longer strong.

Keyword: Intimacy

Absent: The opportunity to be intimate is missing. You don't have a chance to get close to someone. You're not in a relationship right now. A bond is broken. Someone won't go to a deeper level.

Early Phase: You may have a chance to be intimate. A moment of closeness may be approaching. There may be a potential for sharing in the situation. A new relationship may be possible in the future.

Late Phase: The opportunity to be intimate is fading. You passed up a chance to get to know someone. The environment is less personal now. People are no longer willing to bond.

Keyword: Love

Absent: The opportunity to be loving is missing. Your devotion is not encouraged. You can't show affection. Tender moments are few and far between. No one seems to care. Amorous overtures are being rebuffed.

Early Phase: You may have a chance to be loving. Someone may be more open to your advances in the future. A caring gesture may become necessary. An opportunity to forgive may come your way.

Late Phase: The opportunity to be loving is fading. Your attentions are no longer welcome. A chance to show caring has passed. Togetherness is ending. An apology is not easy now.

Two of Cups

Upright

It's a time of connection and joining together. People are working as a unit. A marriage, union, or partnership is in the air. Truce is possible. You can forgive or be forgiven. An attraction exists. A bond is in place.

Reversed

Keyword: Connection

Absent: You're not connected right now. The marriage or other union is not happening. People are not seeing commonalties. Bonds are not being acknowledged. The group has failed to join together.

Early Phase: Connections may be forming. People may be coming together. Tentative links may be created. A marriage or other joining may be coming up. You may need to work with another person. Sharing may become an issue.

Late Phase: The connections are growing thin. There's less togetherness now. The links are dissolving. A marriage has taken place or is unraveling. Relationships are breaking up. You're no longer reaching out to someone.

Keyword: Truce

Absent: There's no truce at the moment. People are not speaking to one another. Opposites are far apart. Peace is not available now. Forgiveness is difficult. No agreement is happening.

Early Phase: Some peace overtures may be considered. A cease-fire may occur at some point. A truce may become possible. You may begin to think about forgiveness. Warring parties may start coming together.

Late Phase: The truce is ending. Peaceful relationships are a thing of the past. The agreement is falling apart. Someone can't let bygones be bygones. Your ability to forgive is fading.

Keyword: Attraction

Absent: You don't feel attracted to someone. You can't generate a positive response. The proposal doesn't appeal to you. You're not inclined to move toward. You're reluctant to get drawn in.

Early Phase: An attraction may be developing. A bond may be forming. Someone or something may pull you in. You may feel more positive in the future.

Late Phase: An attraction is ending. It's hard to imagine what you saw in someone. You no longer feel positive about the matter. The appeal is fading. People have lost interest.

Three of Cups

Upright

It's a time of exuberance and high spirits. Everyone is bursting with energy. Friendship is available. You can trust other people. A community exists. People are helping each other.

Reversed

Keyword: Exuberance

Absent: You're not feeling excited. The energy level is low. There's not much joy. People can't celebrate. The mood is damped down.

Early Phase: You may start to feel more energy. The mood may get lighter in the future. People may feel like celebrating one day. A joyous celebration may be approaching.

Late Phase: There's less excitement now. People are no longer exuberant. You're coming down from your high. The celebration is behind you. The dancing and singing are ending.

Keyword: Friendship

Absent: Friendship is lacking right now. You don't have anyone to confide in. You don't trust others at the moment. Someone is not being hospitable. There's little camaraderie right now.

Early Phase: There may be a potential for friendship. You may get closer to an acquaintance. You may have to rely on a friend in the future. A chance to meet with friends may materialize.

Late Phase: A friendship is breaking up. You can no longer trust someone. There are fewer chances to meet with friends. Your buddies are less important to you now.

Keyword: Community

Absent: There's a lack of community. People are not helping one another. Neighbors are not friendly. Your support group is not available. The team spirit is low. The group bond is not strong.

Early Phase: A community may come together. A team spirit may develop in the future. You may join with like-minded people. There may be a potential for neighbors to get closer. Help may become available.

Late Phase: The community is breaking up. People are losing sight of a common goal. Neighbors are less friendly. You're leaving a support group or team. Bonds are no longer holding.

Four of Cups

Upright

It's a time of self-absorption. Personal concerns are primary. There's a mood of apathy and disengagement. Life seems stale and flat. You're going within. Introspection is important. Someone is withdrawing.

Reversed

Keyword: Self-absorption

Absent: There's a lack of self-absorption. People are not being selfish. Outsiders are not being forgotten. You aren't self-indulgent right now. You're ignoring your own needs at the moment.

Early Phase: You may start focusing on yourself. You may begin to ignore others at some point. Someone may withhold affection in the future. Your areas of concern may start narrowing.

Late Phase: You're becoming less self-absorbed. You're no longer wrapped up in yourself. Egotistical behavior is decreasing. Personal concerns are taking a backseat.

Keyword: Apathy

Absent: Apathy is not evident. People are not losing interest. You're not feeling disengaged. There's no lack of caring. Someone is not being passive. Desire is not gone.

Early Phase: You may lose interest. Desire may disappear in the future. Someday you may not care as much. People may get bored at some point.

Late Phase: The apathy is going away. You're no longer disengaged. The lack of desire is fading. People are not so passive now. Someone is less uncaring.

Keyword: Going Within

Absent: It's impossible to focus within. You have little time for contemplation. Dreams are not being recognized. Your inner life is not flourishing. You don't trust your inner guidance.

Early Phase: You may start focusing on your inner life. Meditation and reflection may become important. Someone may withdraw in the future. Vivid dreams may occur at some point.

Late Phase: Introspection is decreasing. You're having fewer dreams and inner experiences. There's less focus within. Someone is no longer hard to reach.

Five of Cups

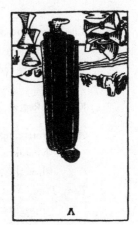

Upright

It's a time of loss and sadness. Goodbyes are in the air. Someone or something is gone. Defeat is a reality. There's a mood of bereavement. A relationship is breaking up. You're feeling regret. A mistake is causing sorrow.

Reversed

Keyword: Loss

Absent: You're not experiencing loss. Nothing is being taken away. Someone is not saying goodbye. People are not losing hope. Defeat is not acknowledged. You're not accepting a loss.

Early Phase: You may experience a loss. Someone may leave in the future. A possession may become vulnerable. There may be a potential for defeat. You may eventually lose hope.

Late Phase: The loss is behind you. You're dealing with a defeat. You experienced a setback. A theft has occurred. You've said your goodbyes. The letting go is ending.

Keyword: Bereavement

Absent: A relationship is not breaking up. You're not feeling alone. Abandonment is not an issue. Grief is not being expressed. A separation is not being acknowledged. Loved ones are not gone.

Early Phase: You may miss someone later. A loved one may depart in the future. A time of bereavement may occur. A mood of sadness may develop. You may be thinking of a possible separation.

Late Phase: The period of bereavement is ending. You're no longer feeling sad. The loved one has departed. The loss of the relationship is behind you. You're feeling less deprived now.

Keyword: Regret

Absent: You're not feeling regret. There's little remorse. People are not sorry. Mistakes are not being acknowledged. You're not having second thoughts.

Early Phase: You may feel regret in the future. Someone may have second thoughts. An apology may become necessary. You may feel remorse someday. Tomorrow you may kick yourself.

Late Phase: You no longer feel regret. Remorse is decreasing. There's little point in crying over spilt milk. You have fewer reservations now.

Six of Cups

Upright

It's a time of good will. People are sharing and offering support. Gifts are available. Innocence is an issue. Someone is unaware. Consciences are clear. There's a focus on childhood and play. A baby is involved.

Reversed

Keyword: Good Will

Absent: You're not experiencing good will. People are not kind and charitable. There's little sharing. A gift is not being offered. Noble impulses are not in evidence.

Early Phase: You may feel good will eventually. Someone may be generous in the future. Good intentions may exist at some point. There may be a potential for sharing. A gift may be forthcoming.

Late Phase: Good will is decreasing. You're no longer feeling accommodating. There's less compassion now. The time for gifts is past. Help is less available now.

Keyword: Innocence

Absent: There's a lack of innocence. Someone's hands are not clean. You're not blind to what's going on. No one appreciates simple joys. An acquittal is not happening.

Early Phase: Innocence may be recognized. Your conscience may clear eventually. An acquittal may be approaching. Someone may be found blameless in the future.

Late Phase: The period of innocence is ending. You're no longer blissfully unaware. There's less resistance to corruption now. The desire to be good is fading. Someone was acquitted.

Keyword: Childhood

Absent: There's little focus on children. A baby or child is not in the picture. Someone is not feeling carefree. Chances to play are rare. You're ignoring childhood associations. Someone is not being taken care of.

Early Phase: A baby or child may become important. A pregnancy or birth may occur. You may get involved with children. There may be a potential for play. Childhood memories may surface.

Late Phase: A pregnancy or birth has occurred. You're no longer focused on children. Playful moments are decreasing. Someone is acting less childish. A baby or child is becoming less central.

Seven of Cups

Upright

It's a time of wishful thinking. You have an elusive dream or hope. Options are available. You can pick and choose. Dissipation and excess are problems. There's a pattern of addiction.

Reversed

Keyword: Wishful Thinking

Absent: You're not kidding yourself. False illusions are not a problem. Your imagination is not running wild. Your idea is not a pipe dream.

Early Phase: Wishful thinking may become a problem. You may lose touch with the truth at some point. Illusions may develop a life of their own. A fantasy may get stronger in the future.

Late Phase: You no longer believe in the dream. The bubble has burst. Hope is fading. The fantasy is less appealing now. You've let go of the illusion.

Keyword: Options

Absent: There are no options right now. The range of choices is limited. You can't afford to be choosy. You're refusing to look at alternatives. Someone is having trouble deciding.

Early Phase: Options may increase at some point. You may have more choices in the future. More possibilities may develop. Your vision may expand.

Late Phase: Your choices have narrowed. There are fewer options now. People can no longer pick and choose. Some possibilities have been removed. You eliminated some alternatives.

Keyword: Dissipation

Absent: You're not overindulging. Excess is being avoided. Laziness is not a problem. Someone is not procrastinating. Your health is not at risk. Addictions are not being acknowledged.

Early Phase: Laziness may become a problem. Loose living may start to be attractive. You may let everything go in the future. The environment may get disorganized. An addiction may develop.

Late Phase: The dissipation is ending. You're no longer overindulging. The addiction is coming under control. You're less disorganized now. The carousing is ending.

Eight of Cups

Upright

It's a time of deeper meaning. Values and personal truths are important. Someone is moving on. There's a need to disentangle. A journey is beginning. Weariness is a problem. People are burned out.

Reversed

Keyword: Deeper Meaning

Absent: The deeper meaning is not apparent. No one is looking for the truth. You're not concentrating on what's important. You're not avoiding the rat race. Your spirituality is being neglected.

Early Phase: You may start seeking deeper meaning. A hunger for truth may develop. A journey of discovery may begin in the future. Spiritual matters may become important. The atmosphere may turn serious.

Late Phase: You're less concerned with meaning now. Honest answers no longer matter. The serious tone is disappearing. People are forgetting what's important. Your spiritual yearnings are fading.

Keyword: Moving On

Absent: Someone is not moving on. You can't break free. Someone doesn't understand the need to let go. You can't leave a hopeless situation. Your trip is not getting off the ground.

Early Phase: You may need to move on in the future. The time to let go may be approaching. Someone may decide to walk away. You may abandon the situation.

Late Phase: Someone has moved on. You've removed yourself from the problem. A door has closed. You've said your goodbyes. A phase is ending. You no longer need to move on.

Keyword: Weariness

Absent: You're not tired right now. There's no lack of energy. Burnout is not a problem. Demands are not too draining. You're not dragging through the day.

Early Phase: You may become fatigued. Someone may grow tired of the situation. Worry may consume you in the future. Burnout may become an issue. A struggle may eventually wear you out.

Late Phase: Lack of energy is no longer a problem. The weight of the world has been lifted off your shoulders. You feel less tired now. The risk of burnout is ending. The mood of resignation is lifting.

Nine of Cups

Upright

It's a time of wish fulfillment. You're achieving your heart's desire. Dreams are coming true. Satisfaction is yours. The situation is working out the way you want. Sensual pleasure is a delightful focus.

Reversed

Keyword: Wish Fulfillment

Absent: Your wish is not coming true. You're not getting what you think you want. Goals are being thwarted. Results don't match desires. The dream is not a reality.

Early Phase: You may realize your heart's desire. A goal may get closer. Someone's wish may be granted in the future. A prayer may be answered.

Late Phase: The time for getting your wish is past. You're no longer focused on a dream. Achieving your goal is less important now. Your desire is fading.

Keyword: Satisfaction

Absent: You're not satisfied. Results are not to your liking. Someone is put out. There's no pleasing some people. Contentment is low. You're not feeling smug right now.

Early Phase: You may become satisfied. The situation may get better. There may be a potential for contentment. You may be pleased with your results in the future.

Late Phase: You're less satisfied now. The situation is no longer gratifying. Contentment is on the decline. Someone has upset the apple cart. People are not as smug as they were.

Keyword: Sensual Pleasure

Absent: You can't enjoy your senses. You have to forego pleasure. There are few opportunities to enjoy sex. Your body is constrained in some way. Beauty is not appreciated. Luxury is not an option. There's little focus on the arts.

Early Phase: You may begin seeking pleasure. A chance to enjoy your senses may come up. A sexual encounter may occur. You may have more luxury in the future.

Late Phase: Your focus on pleasure is decreasing. Sensual experiences are less common now. Sex is no longer as central. Surroundings are not as delightful. You can't afford to indulge at the same level.

Ten of Cups

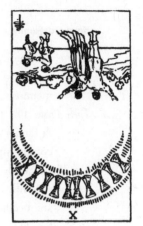

Upright

It's a time of joy and good fortune. Emotional fulfillment is yours. Love is all around you. Happiness is available. Peace is in the air. The environment is calm. Family is important.

Reversed

Keyword: Joy

Absent: There is little joy right now. Happiness is elusive. You lack a sense of well-being. Someone can't express love openly. Good fortune is hard to come by.

Early Phase: You may feel joy soon. Moments of happiness may start to occur. There may be a potential for love. The future may be brighter. A more positive outlook may develop.

Late Phase: Your happiness is fading. There's less joy in the air. It's getting harder to count your blessings. The period of good fortune is past. Love is no longer strong.

Keyword: Peace

Absent: There's a lack of peace. The truce is broken. People are not friendly toward one another. Your serenity is disturbed. Someone is ill at ease. The environment is not harmonious.

Early Phase: A movement toward peace may start. An accord may become possible. Warring parties may begin talking. You may become calmer and more relaxed. Harmony may return in the future.

Late Phase: The peace is ending. The time for reconciliation has passed. There's less desire for agreement now. The tranquil mood is evaporating. You're no longer responding calmly.

Keyword: Family

Absent: The family is disrupted. A family event is not going smoothly. A relative is having difficulty. Someone in the family is not included. Family members are not seeing eye-to-eye.

Early Phase: The family may come together. Family harmony may be possible. A family matter may be resolved soon. A family celebration may be coming up.

Late Phase: Family togetherness is declining. Someone has shaken up the family. A family celebration has ended or was unable to occur. Family matters are becoming less important. You're no longer connected to your family.

Page of Cups

Upright

Cups' energy is available to help you move in a new direction. The call to be emotional, intuitive, intimate, and loving is strong right now. Take this chance to go beyond your usual limits and habits!

Reversed

Keywords: Be Emotional, Be Intuitive, Be Intimate, Be Loving

Absent: The time is NOT right, or you CAN'T follow the call to:
> show your feelings, let your heart lead the way, express your sentiments, be moved, receive inner guidance, act on a hunch, trust your gut, sense the undercurrents, start or renew a love affair, get close to someone, go beyond formalities, move closer, forgive, respond with caring, avoid judgments, open your heart.

Early Phase: The time MAY BE APPROACHING when you'll have a chance to:
> be romantic, shed detachment, cry or grieve, let the anger out, remember your dreams, pick up unspoken signals, be clairvoyant, trust your inner knowing, remove personal barriers, share something personal, make love, initiate sex, make a thoughtful gesture, feel sympathy, mend a broken relationship, hug.

Late Phase: The time is ENDING for any chance to:
> feel joy, put feelings first, wear your heart on your sleeve, respond to beauty, be psychic, rely on guesses, read someone's mind, trust your sixth sense, provide confidential information, show warmth, share secrets, be personal, be understanding, show deep affection, turn away wrath, support unconditionally.

Knight of Cups

Upright

Cups' energy is extra strong. You, someone else, or the situation may be romantic, imaginative, sensitive, refined, and introspective OR overemotional, fanciful, temperamental, overrefined, and introverted.

Reversed

Keywords (Positive): Romantic, Imaginative, Sensitive, Refined

Keywords (Negative): Overemotional, Fanciful, Temperamental, Introverted

Absent: You or someone else is NOT:
idealizing love, emphasizing emotions, showing imagination, sharing a vision, demonstrating deep caring, empathizing, honoring beauty, creating a pleasing environment, valuing the inner life, seeing into the heart OR showing jealousy, acting melodramatically, indulging in daydreams, shading the truth, experiencing mood swings, brooding, avoiding unpleasantness, getting overwhelmed, exaggerating failings, being driven to self-examination.

Early Phase: You or another person MAY BEGIN to:
enjoy the poetry of life, feel romantic, delve into the unconscious, avoid the ordinary, show sensitivity, be diplomatic, look for the finest, be more refined, seek self-improvement, try to understand OR be overemotional, blow hot and cold, let your imagination run wild, sulk, take offense easily, be finicky, focus on style over substance, be too introspective, become self-absorbed.

Late Phase: You or another person is NO LONGER:

remembering special moments, sharing feelings, using imagination, looking beyond the obvious, understanding another's pain, being discrete, acting with refinement, being gracious, looking within, being introspective OR being gushy, giving in to excess, indulging in fancies, focusing on big ideas that come to nothing, getting very depressed, being temperamental, being overly fussy, leaving when the going gets rough, concerned only with self, obsessed with personal issues.

Queen of Cups

Upright

Cups' energy is present as a state of being. A mood that is loving, tenderhearted, intuitive, psychic, and spiritual is evident. You or someone else is adopting or could adopt the mood of a lover, comforter, compassionate friend, psychic, intuitive, medium, spiritual guide, or minister.

Reversed

Keywords: Loving, Tenderhearted, Intuitive, Psychic, Spiritual

Absent: The mood of you or someone else is NOT:
>loving, accepting, sensitive, gentle, intuitive, guided by the heart, tuned in, reverent, spiritual.

Early Phase: The mood of you or someone else MAY BECOME:
>patient, caring, compassionate, kind, guided by trust, sympathetic, in communion, devotional, ecstatic.

Late Phase: The mood of you or someone else is NO LONGER:
>tender, affectionate, merciful, humane, solicitous, responsive, simpatico, devotional, joyful, blissful.

King of Cups

Upright

Cups' energy is present in an active, outgoing way. Actions that are wise, calm, diplomatic, caring, and tolerant are evident. You or someone else is acting or could act as a guide, counselor, healer, caring friend, wise teacher, caregiver, or mediator.

Reversed

Keywords: Wise, Calm, Diplomatic, Caring, Tolerant

Absent: You or someone else is NOT:

> taking wise actions, giving good advice, calming tensions, keeping your head in a crisis, being tactful, diffusing a stressful situation, showing you care, helping someone in need, giving others their freedom, avoiding prejudice.

Early Phase: You or someone else MAY BEGIN to:

> act with more awareness, demonstrate sound judgment, soothe ruffled feathers, provide a quieting influence, keep everyone together, mediate, provide healing, show compassion, accept limitations, respond patiently.

Late Phase: You or someone else is NO LONGER:

> teaching wisely, helping constructively, staying composed, providing stability, staying balanced, showing diplomacy, volunteering, responding to a call for help, looking the other way, tolerating misdeeds.

Ace of Swords

Upright

Swords' air energy is at your disposal right now. There's an opportunity to use mental force. You can expand your experience of fortitude, justice, and truth.

Reversed

Keyword: Mental Force

Absent: The opportunity to use mental force is missing. You lack an outlet for your intelligence. There's no chance to learn the facts. People are not being logical. Your ideas are not being heard.

Early Phase: You may have a chance to use mental force. You may be able to express your thoughts. Someone may become reasonable in the future. You may need to be more objective.

Late Phase: The opportunity to use mental force is fading. There are fewer intellectual challenges now. The chance to share your ideas is past. The time for thinking of a solution is ending. You no longer trust your analysis.

Keyword: Fortitude

Absent: The opportunity to show fortitude is missing. No one is letting you try. Your persistence is not appreciated. There's little adversity right now. Obstacles are few. People are not enduring.

Early Phase: You may have to show fortitude. Your resolve may be tested in the future. You may need to face your problems. An obstacle may be on the horizon. You may require inner strength.

Late Phase: The opportunity to show fortitude is fading. The test of your endurance is ending. The obstacle has been worked around. Setbacks are no longer a problem. The need for courage is no longer strong.

Keyword: Justice

Absent: The opportunity to be just is missing. You're not being treated fairly. No one supports your cause. People are not staying impartial. An equitable solution is not happening.

Early Phase: You may get a chance to be just. You may need to focus on what's fair. You may be offered an equal shot. Someone may try to make up for a past wrong. A matter of principle may come up.

Late Phase: The opportunity to be just is fading. You can no longer correct a mistake. The support for fair play is ending. You're less focused on doing what's right. Someone has revealed bias or prejudice.

Keyword: Truth

Absent: The opportunity to be truthful is missing. Honesty is not being encouraged. You're not allowed to say what you think. People can't let go of illusions. The facts are being ignored. You're resisting the urge to confess.

Early Phase: You may have a chance to be truthful. You may decide to be honest. Someone may open up to the facts. Your sincerity may be acknowledged. A revealing encounter may be coming up.

Late Phase: The opportunity to be truthful is fading. It's not as easy to be honest now. A chance to put everything on the table has passed. People no longer want to face reality. Someone has refused to confess.

Two of Swords

Upright

It's a time of blocked emotions. Feelings are being repressed. You're hiding some distress. Avoidance is a factor. People are choosing not to know. The situation is at a stalemate. Everyone is stuck.

Reversed

Keyword: Blocked Emotions

Absent: Emotions are not blocked at the moment. People are not hiding their feelings. Defenses are not working. It's hard to keep your distance. The usual restraints are not in place.

Early Phase: You may start shutting down emotionally. Your heart may become hardened. You may hide your feelings. Walls may begin to form. Someone may become distant and cool.

Late Phase: You're unblocking your emotions. The ice is beginning to melt. Someone is less defensive now. You can no longer bottle up your feelings.

Keyword: Avoidance

Absent: You're not avoiding the truth. Pretending is not possible now. Choosing ignorance is not an option. People are not skirting the issues.

Early Phase: You may begin avoiding someone. Someone may start ignoring a problem. An unpleasantness may be swept under the rug. People may start pretending.

Late Phase: You can no longer avoid the situation. You've decided to stop pretending. People are less inclined to ignore the truth. It's no longer necessary to keep up a show.

Keyword: Stalemate

Absent: There's no stalemate at the moment. You're not stuck, despite appearances. A resolution is not out of the question. People are not afraid to act or make a decision.

Early Phase: A stalemate may develop. Positions may become fixed in place. Options may begin disappearing. You may be heading toward an impasse. It may get harder to maneuver in the future.

Late Phase: The stalemate is dissolving. People are no longer fixed in their positions. There's less fear of making a move. You're less reluctant to rock the boat.

Three of Swords

Upright

It's a time of heartbreak and disappointment. You or someone you know is hurting inside. Loneliness is a reality. You feel isolated from loved ones. Betrayal is in the air. A painful truth is being revealed.

Reversed

Keyword: Heartbreak

Absent: You're not suffering right now. No one's feelings are being hurt. There are no heartbreaking moments. The situation is not disappointing.

Early Phase: You may suffer pain in the future. You may be heading toward some heartbreak. You may begin feeling vulnerable emotionally. You may hurt someone in the future.

Late Phase: The heartbreak is behind you. The pain is dulling somewhat. You're coming to terms with your disappointment. You're no longer hurting someone.

Keyword: Loneliness

Absent: Loneliness is not a problem right now. You don't feel isolated or separated from others. There's no overt rejection. You haven't been deserted.

Early Phase: You may begin feeling lonely. A time of separation may be approaching. You may decide to reject someone or be rejected. Your friends and loved ones may start pulling away.

Late Phase: You're no longer feeling lonely. Loved ones are less distant. A separation is ending. You're putting a rejection behind you. Isolation is becoming less of a problem.

Keyword: Betrayal

Absent: There's no betrayal for now. You're not being let down. The back-stabbing is not occurring. No one is taking actions against you at the moment.

Early Phase: You may begin feeling less trustful. You may be betrayed in the future. Someone may turn against you. You may start seeing signs of dishonesty. You may break your word or vows.

Late Phase: A betrayal has passed. The period of lying and deceit is ending. The painful revelations are behind you. You let someone down but have resolved to mend your ways.

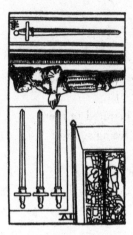

Four of Swords

Upright

It's a time of rest and recovery. You can heal by enjoying peace and relaxation. Moments of contemplation are important. There is time to think and reflect. Quiet preparation for the future is vital.

Reversed

Keyword: Rest

Absent: There's no time for rest and relaxation. Peaceful moments are not available. You can't find the time for healing. You're not taking the breaks you need.

Early Phase: The pace may start to slow. You may need to take a break soon. A rest period may be approaching. You may have an opportunity to relax.

Late Phase: Your break period is ending. Your recovery is almost complete. The pace is no longer slow. Moments of peace and quiet are less frequent now.

Keyword: Contemplation

Absent: There's no time to think. People are not looking at the situation thoughtfully. You're not examining your motivations. No one is making an in-depth analysis.

Early Phase: A time for reflection may be approaching. You may need to stop and think things over. You may withdraw from the action for a time.

Late Phase: A period of contemplation is ending. You no longer need time alone to think. Your meditation is coming to an end. The thoughtful moments are decreasing.

Keyword: Quiet Preparation

Absent: No preparations are being made. There is no readiness. The situation is not stable. You're not in a position to handle whatever comes up.

Early Phase: You may begin preparations. Someone may be getting ready behind the scenes. You may need to secure your base in the future. Planning may become vital.

Late Phase: The preparation phase is over. You no longer need to secure the situation. You did what you needed to do. There's less focus on planning now.

Five of Swords

Upright

It's a time of self-interest. People are putting their own needs first. There's a mood of hostility. Discord is evident. Everyone is taking sides. Open dishonor is a factor. Shady dealings are being exposed.

Reversed

Keyword: Self-Interest

Absent: You're not acting in your own self-interest. The mood is not openly selfish. No one is pushing a personal agenda. The needs of the group are not being ignored.

Early Phase: You may need to put yourself first. Selfishness may become more obvious. Someone may initiate a power play. A dog-eat-dog environment may develop.

Late Phase: There's less selfishness now. People are no longer self-absorbed. The blatant power plays are ending. The "me-first" mood is decreasing.

Keyword: Discord

Absent: There's no hostility at the moment. People are not fighting. The environment is not mean and nasty. People are not showing anger or ill will.

Early Phase: The fighting may resume. A mood of ill will may develop. The environment may get nasty. A battle may be brewing. You may become angry and out of sorts. People may start to take sides.

Late Phase: The conflict is ending. The environment is no longer openly hostile. The ill will is fading. There's less anger and shouting. The biggest battle is behind you.

Keyword: Open Dishonor

Absent: There's no open dishonor. No criminal activity is going on. You're not losing sight of what's right. Integrity is not being sacrificed at the moment.

Early Phase: You may begin losing your moral compass. You may be thinking of an illegal or unsavory act. Criminal activity may be exposed in the future. A test of integrity may be approaching. You may be tempted to take the low road.

Late Phase: A test of your integrity is behind you. Obvious dishonors are decreasing. You're no longer tempted to cheat. Criminal activity is in the past. The unsavory atmosphere is fading.

Six of Swords

Upright

It's time for the blues. Your energy and passion are low, but recovery is in progress. You're moving to a more positive place. Travel is a factor. A change of scene is in the air.

Reversed

Keyword: The Blues

Absent: You don't feel too sad or depressed. The blues are not a problem right now. You aren't feeling low or weighed down by concerns. You won't allow yourself to feel sad.

Early Phase: You may become depressed. You may be heading toward a low period. Life may begin losing its sparkle. You may need to face your sadness.

Late Phase: You're no longer sad. The mood of depression is lifting. You're putting the blues behind you. Your energy is returning. You're no longer discouraged.

Keyword: Recovery

Absent: You can't focus on recovery right now. You can't acknowledge the need to heal. People are not dealing with the aftermath of trauma. Coping mechanisms are not in place.

Early Phase: A time of healing may be approaching. You may have to focus on recovery. The aftereffects may become noticeable. You may begin mending.

Late Phase: The recovery period is ending. The healing process is behind you. The shock of the trauma is no longer as severe. Your convalescence is coming to an end.

Keyword: Travel

Absent: There's little travel. You're not moving to a new place. The current mood or scene is not changing. No one is being uprooted. A trip is not in the works.

Early Phase: You may have to leave on a trip. Someone may be planning a move. A change of scene may be coming up. An opportunity to travel may materialize. An inner journey may start.

Late Phase: You're returning from a trip. A move is behind you. You've taken an inner journey. A change of scene has been nearly completed. Travel is less likely now.

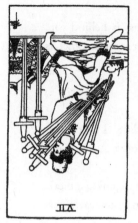

Seven of Swords

Upright

Someone is leaving or running away. Responsibilities are being avoided. Procrastination is a problem. A lone-wolf style is in evidence. People are taking solitary actions. Hidden dishonors are a factor. There is dishonesty behind the scenes.

Reversed

Keyword: Running Away

Absent: No one is leaving. People are not taking the easy way out. There's little desire to sneak off. You're not shirking your obligations.

Early Phase: You may be thinking about leaving. You may shirk a responsibility. Someone may try to sneak off. You may want to run away at some point.

Late Phase: You're no longer running away. The desire to escape is not so strong. There's less procrastination. Avoidance is decreasing.

Keyword: Lone-Wolf Style

Absent: You're unable to act on your own. Being solitary is not an option. You can't handle everything yourself. A lone-wolf style is not being encouraged.

Early Phase: You may need to be alone in the future. You may be thinking of going solo. People may drift apart. A mood of alienation may develop. Independence may become attractive.

Late Phase: The lone wolf is rejoining the pack. People are no longer acting in isolation. Your desire for independence is fading. The need to stay apart is ending. Independent action is less acceptable now.

Keyword: Hidden Dishonor

Absent: There are no hidden dishonors at the moment. No one is deceiving or being deceived. People are not hiding shameful secrets. Undercover manipulations are not a factor.

Early Phase: You may do something unworthy. You may head down a slippery slope. Someone may lie or cheat in the future. A crime or unpleasantness may be covered up.

Late Phase: Dishonorable acts are decreasing. You're extricating yourself from a dubious situation. You no longer want to live without integrity. You're putting the lies and cheating behind you. A shady past is less important now.

Eight of Swords

Upright

It's a time of restriction and limitation. You're feeling trapped by circumstances. Few options seem available. There's confusion and lack of direction. No one's clear on the issues. Feelings of powerlessness are strong.

Reversed

Keyword: Restriction

Absent: You're not feeling restricted or tied down. There's no lack of options. No one is being persecuted. Obstacles are not a problem.

Early Phase: You may start feeling hemmed in. Restrictions may be put in place. There may be fewer choices in the future. Oppression may become a problem. The walls may begin closing in.

Late Phase: Restrictions are decreasing. You're feeling less confined. There are fewer obstacles in your way now. Oppression is ending. Freedom no longer seems impossible.

Keyword: Confusion

Absent: There's no uncertainty right now. People are not confused about what's happening. You're not feeling overwhelmed. Lack of direction is not a problem.

Early Phase: You may become uncertain. Confusion may increase. People may start floundering and lose purpose. Mixed messages may be sent at some point.

Late Phase: There's less uncertainty now. You no longer feel so overwhelmed. The period of confusion is behind you. Lack of direction is ceasing to be a problem.

Keyword: Powerlessness

Absent: You're not feeling victimized. Lack of power is not a factor. There's no need to seek rescue. Your hands are not tied.

Early Phase: You may lose power. Weakness may become a problem. People may start feeling vulnerable. Someone may become feeble or incapacitated.

Late Phase: You're no longer feeling like a victim. Doubts about your power are almost gone. Feelings of helplessness are fading. People are no longer immobilized.

Nine of Swords

Upright

It's a time of worry and anxiety. Everyone is feeling tense. Feelings of guilt are strong. Someone is filled with regret. You're experiencing some anguish and moments of despair.

Reversed

Keyword: Worry

Absent: You have few misgivings about the situation. Worry is not a problem. There's little anxiety at the moment. There's no immediate cause for concern.

Early Phase: You may begin worrying. Some problems may preoccupy you in the future. You may have trouble sleeping. People may become apprehensive. Some anxious moments may be coming up.

Late Phase: You're worrying less now. The situation no longer seems troubling. Anxious moments are decreasing. Everyone seems less upset.

Keyword: Guilt

Absent: No one is guilty. There's little regret or remorse. Someone is not acknowledging guilt. You don't feel the need to punish yourself. Sin is not an issue.

Early Phase: You may feel guilty. You may have trouble forgiving yourself. Feelings of remorse may develop. You may experience regret in the future. Someone may be found guilty.

Late Phase: The guilt is decreasing. You're no longer being hard on yourself. There's less cause for regret now. The time for remorse is ending. A guilty verdict has been declared.

Keyword: Anguish

Absent: You're not depressed at the moment. The atmosphere is not gloomy. Despair is not being expressed. No one seems to be discouraged. You're not feeling despondent.

Early Phase: You may begin to despair. You may start crying more often. Painful memories may begin to surface. Someone may become depressed. The mood may get darker.

Late Phase: The anguish is fading. The dark times are behind you. The depression is lifting. You've been through a dark night of the soul.

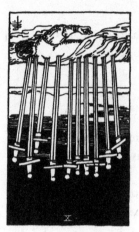

Ten of Swords

Upright

You're bottoming out. The situation is as bad as it's going to get. Victim mentality is a problem. You're feeling persecuted. Martyrdom is in the air. A sacrifice is being considered.

Reversed

Keyword: Bottoming Out

Absent: You haven't hit rock bottom. Matters are not hopeless. You're not allowing the worst to happen. Someone can't accept the seriousness of the situation.

Early Phase: A low period may be developing. Events may start going from bad to worse. You may enter a downward spiral. There may be some backsliding in the future.

Late Phase: The lowest point is behind you. You weathered the storm, and now the skies are clearing. You hit rock bottom but managed to pull through. The discouraging signs are fading.

Keyword: Victim Mentality

Absent: You're not feeling like a victim. There are no signs of self-pity. Attacks are not occurring. People are not feeling persecuted. Loss of power is not a problem.

Early Phase: You may begin feeling like a victim. Someone may start indulging in self-pity. Attacks may become more frequent. You may suspect someone is targeting you. The victim role may become more central.

Late Phase: The situation seems less threatening. The attacks are decreasing. You're no longer on the receiving end. The period of powerlessness is ending.

Keyword: Martyrdom

Absent: There's no need to play the martyr. A sacrifice is not necessary. People are not letting themselves be walked on. The time is not right to make a stand.

Early Phase: You may start feeling like a doormat. Others may begin taking advantage. You may need to sacrifice in the future. Someone may be martyred for a principle. A mood of resignation may set in.

Late Phase: The martyr role is fading. You no longer need to put others first. The time of sacrifice is ending. There's less need to take a backseat now. The ordeal of suffering is behind you.

Page of Swords

Upright

Swords' energy is available to help you move in a new direction. The call to use your mind, have fortitude, and be truthful and just is strong right now. The Page of Swords often represents a moment of challenge. Take this chance to go beyond your usual limits and habits!

Reversed

Keywords: Use Your Mind, Be Truthful, Be Just, Have Fortitude

Absent: The time is NOT right, or you CAN'T follow the call to:
develop a plan, think clearly, get to the heart of the matter, analyze the situation, be honest, speak your mind, face the facts, avoid deceit, do what's fair, treat others equally, accept responsibility, right a wrong, keep your resolve, try repeatedly, hang tough, refuse to quit.

Early Phase: The time MAY BE APPROACHING when you'll have a chance to:
be logical, examine your beliefs, do what's smart, outthink the other person, clear up confusion, give up lies, stop fooling yourself, admit there's a problem, act with principle, champion a cause, do what's right, accept the consequences, push past discouragement, get back on the horse, endure, outlast others.

Late Phase: The time is ENDING for any chance to:
use your wits, figure out the solution, solve the puzzle, draw the right conclusions, be frank and open, stick to the facts, present an accurate picture, confess, stay impartial, avoid prejudice, honor fair play, stick to the law, be determined, show some spunk, test your mettle, stay firm.

Knight of Swords

Upright

Swords' energy is extra strong. You, someone else, or the situation may be direct, authoritative, incisive, knowledge-able, and logical OR blunt, overbearing, cutting, opinion-ated, and unfeeling.

Reversed

Keywords (Positive): Direct, Authoritative, Incisive, Knowledgeable, Logical

Keywords (Negative): Blunt, Overbearing, Cutting, Opinionated, Unfeeling

Absent: You or someone else is NOT:

being outspoken, getting right to the point, speaking with assurance, arguing a case forcefully, being incisive, demonstrating a keen intellect, becoming well-informed, finding out what's going on, using logic to good purpose, analyzing the situation OR speaking without tact, being brusque, becoming domineering, forcing a position on others, using too much sarcasm, being overly critical, lacking tolerance, coming across as arrogant, treating people like numbers, staying too aloof.

Early Phase: You or another person MAY:

speak your mind, be frank, command attention, act with certainty, get to the core issue, break through confusion, be sought as an expert, know the answers, reason clearly, set aside emotional factors OR be rude, disregard the feelings of others, expect immediate compliance, dominate the situation, be overbearing, indulge in put-downs, become closed minded, ignore other viewpoints, dismiss intuition, get cut off from feelings.

Late Phase: You or another person is NO LONGER:

being straightforward, talking candidly, acting decisively, being a reliable source of information, expressing ideas succinctly, staying sharp and alert, staying knowledgeable, offering useful information, thinking rationally, being systematic OR being curt with others, wielding a sharp tongue, acting like a tyrant, squelching dissent, using a barbed wit, belittling associates, needing to have the last word, being dogmatic, ignoring suffering, acting cold and uncaring.

Queen of Swords

Upright

Swords' energy is present as a state of being. A mood that is honest, astute, forthright, witty, and experienced is evident. You or someone else is adopting or could adopt the mood of a wit, comedian, trickster, con man, cynic, skeptic, whistle-blower, straight shooter, coach, critic, or advisor.

Reversed

Keywords: Honest, Astute, Forthright, Witty, Experienced

Absent: The mood of you or someone else is NOT:

> honest, fair, smart, discerning, direct, straightforward, funny, clever, experienced, knowing.

Early Phase: The mood of you or someone else MAY BECOME:

> open, truthful, perceptive, insightful, frank, candid, playful, amusing, worldly, quick on the uptake.

Late Phase: The mood of you or someone else is NO LONGER:

> realistic, authentic, clear sighted, aware, plain speaking, forthright, quick, sharp, cynical, jaded.

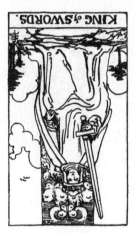

King of Swords

Upright

Swords' energy is present in an active, outgoing way. Actions that are intellectual, analytical, articulate, just, and ethical are important. You or someone else is acting or could act as a teacher, mentor, thinker, philosopher, theorizer, researcher, writer, translator, speaker, spokesperson, judge, or referee.

Reversed

Keywords: Intellectual, Analytical, Articulate, Just, Ethical

Absent: You or someone else is NOT:

thinking carefully, grasping the concepts, acting rationally, arguing, communicating well, speaking with authority, staying objective, judging wisely, encouraging high standards, acting ethically.

Early Phase: You or someone else MAY BEGIN to:

conduct research, teach or learn, become involved in a game, apply logic, write, learn a language, tell the truth, take up a cause, shun corruption, take the high road.

Late Phase: You or someone else is NO LONGER:

using your mind, inspiring with ideas, dealing with complexity, analyzing the problem, articulating your position, telling it like it is, honoring all sides of an issue, doing what's fair, sticking to principles, acting honorably.

Ace of Pentacles

Upright

Pentacles' earth energy is at your disposal right now. There's an opportunity to use material force. You can expand your experience of prosperity, practicality, and trust.

Reversed

Keyword: Material Force

Absent: The opportunity to use material force is missing. You lack a physical outlet. There's no chance to make a real-world impact. People are not focused on results. Your body or health is not strong.

Early Phase: You may have a chance to use material force. Physical strength may become necessary. Ideas may become more tangible. You may need to be more concrete. The natural world may become important.

Late Phase: The opportunity to use material force is fading. There are fewer physical challenges now. The chance to build something real is past. People are less interested in results. The environment is no longer being protected.

Keyword: Prosperity

Absent: The opportunity to be prosperous is missing. Chances to invest are lacking. Your efforts are not being rewarded. You're not reaching your stated goals. The environment is not conducive to growth.

Early Phase: You may have a chance for prosperity. A chance to invest may come up. The financial environment may improve in the future. Your assets may start to increase. You may get the support you need.

Late Phase: The opportunity to be prosperous is fading. An investment offer has been withdrawn. Chances to make money are no longer common. The climate of abundance is ending. Spending can't be as free now.

Keyword: Practicality

Absent: The opportunity to be practical is missing. Realistic plans are not being considered. No one is showing much common sense. You're not staying grounded. People are not focused on what will work.

Early Phase: You may have a chance to be practical. A realistic solution may materialize. You may need to focus on the tools at hand. Someone may become more down to earth. A real-world concern may come up.

Late Phase: The opportunity to be practical is fading. There's less support for the reasonable choice. Being sensible is no longer valued. The common-sense approach is being discarded.

Keyword: Trust

Absent: The opportunity to trust or be trusted is missing. Someone is not telling the truth. You can't accept the situation at face value. Someone doesn't believe you. You can't prove your case. Confidences are not being kept.

Early Phase: You may have a chance to trust or be trusted. Someone may ask you to believe. Your reliability may be tested at some point. Someone may depend on you in the future.

Late Phase: The opportunity to trust or be trusted is fading. Someone no longer has faith in you. Your word is not good enough anymore. Your desire to believe is nearly gone. You're not as gullible as you were.

Two of Pentacles

Upright

It's a time of juggling. You must balance many demands. The situation is flexible and open to change. New directions are available. There is fun, laughter, and good times. All can be accomplished with great gusto.

Reversed

Keyword: Juggling

Absent: There's no need to juggle right now. You're not in a busy period. The pace is not hectic. Someone can't manage all the tasks. Balance is not being maintained.

Early Phase: There may be more demands in the future. A busy period may lie ahead. You may need to cover all the bases. Balance may become important.

Late Phase: The busy time is ending. You no longer have to struggle for balance. Demands were handled; now the pace is slowing. There's less need to juggle now.

Keyword: Flexible

Absent: The situation is not flexible. There's little openness to new approaches. You don't have room to maneuver. Someone is not adapting to changes.

Early Phase: There may be more flexibility in the future. You may be able to adapt. Someone may open to change. New options may develop at some point.

Late Phase: There's less flexibility now. You're no longer open to change. Your options are narrowing. The alternatives are disappearing.

Keyword: Fun

Absent: There's little fun right now. People are not enjoying themselves. You can't do what gives you pleasure. It's hard to see the humor in the situation.

Early Phase: A party or celebration may be coming up. You may have more fun in the future. There may be more opportunities for play. Good times may be on the way.

Late Phase: The fun is ending. People are no longer enjoying themselves. You have less time for play. A party or celebration has passed. The laughter is fading.

Three of Pentacles

Upright

The time is right for teamwork. People are working together cooperatively. The focus is on planning and preparation. Competence is important. You're handling your tasks well. Everything is moving forward smoothly.

Reversed

Keyword: Teamwork

Absent: There's little teamwork. People are not functioning as a unit. Coordination is lacking. There's no spirit of cooperation. Someone refuses to join with others.

Early Phase: You may become part of a team. There may be potential for cooperation. The group may come together in the future. A spirit of camaraderie may develop.

Late Phase: A team is breaking up. People are no longer functioning as a unit. Everyone is starting to go separate ways. There's less coordination and cooperation.

Keyword: Planning

Absent: There's no planning. People are not following a schedule. Preparations are lacking. You're not thinking about the future. No one is focused on what's to come.

Early Phase: You may make a plan. You may get organized at some point. The preparation stage may begin. A schedule may be implemented in the future.

Late Phase: There's less planning now. The schedule is slipping. The details are no longer being worked out. The preparation stage is ending. Your orderly projections are less reliable.

Keyword: Competence

Absent: Competence is lacking. The job is not being handled well. Goals are not getting met. You're not sure you can handle the situation successfully.

Early Phase: Someone may be more competent in the future. The system may start to work. People may begin handling their assignments better. You may find the skills you need.

Late Phase: The job is no longer getting done properly. Tasks are being neglected. You're losing confidence in your abilities. You have less faith in the system.

Four of Pentacles

Upright

It's a time of possessiveness. Issues of ownership are important. There's a mood of enforced stability. Someone is showing a need to control. You're blocking change or meeting resistance to change. Stagnation is a problem.

Reversed

Keyword: Possessiveness

Absent: There's little sense of ownership. Greed and jealousy are not a problem. You're not involved with staking claim or getting your share. You're denying a desire to possess.

Early Phase: You may become possessive. Jealousy or greed may develop. You may need to protect what you have. Someone may try to stake a claim.

Late Phase: You're less concerned with holding on. A focus on ownership is decreasing. There's no longer reason to be possessive. Jealousy is diminishing. People are less tied down.

Keyword: Control

Absent: There's no control. Few limits and restrictions are in place. The situation lacks direction. No one is keeping order. You have little structure in your life. There's no attempt to constrain you.

Early Phase: A need for order may develop. Limits and rules may become necessary. You may be asked to step in and take charge. There may be more structure in the future.

Late Phase: The structure in place is breaking up. Rules are no longer being followed. There is less control now. The level of organization is decreasing. You're losing your handle on the situation.

Keyword: Blocking Change

Absent: There are no blocks to change. Impediments do not exist. The way forward is not obscured. No obstacle is holding you back. No one is standing in your way.

Early Phase: A period of stagnation may be coming. Obstructions may occur. Resistance may become a problem. You may encounter roadblocks.

Late Phase: Blocks to change are decreasing. Resistance is fading. You're less opposed to new ideas and approaches. People are no longer committed to the status quo.

Five of Pentacles

Upright

Hard times are here. You're struggling with financial and practical problems. Ill health is a concern. Care of your body and its needs is important. Rejection or disapproval is an issue. Someone is being kept on the outside.

Reversed

Keyword: Hard Times

Absent: There's no lack of money. You're not having material problems. No one is in want right now. People do not need to struggle. Survival is not an issue.

Early Phase: Signs of financial trouble may develop. Hard times may be approaching. A period of lack may be on the horizon. You may feel insecure in the future.

Late Phase: The worse times are behind you. You no longer have to struggle so hard. There are fewer financial concerns. Practical problems are decreasing.

Keyword: Ill Health

Absent: Your health is not a problem right now. There are no symptoms at the moment. Sickness is not an issue. Someone is in remission. Your physical condition is not poor.

Early Phase: A health concern may develop in the future. A physical problem may show up. Your body may send you warning signs. You may start feeling weak. Stress and tension may become a problem.

Late Phase: The health crisis is behind you. A medical problem is less serious. You no longer feel run down and weak. Stress levels are decreasing. The symptoms are disappearing.

Keyword: Rejection

Absent: You're not being rejected. No one is being excluded. A dismissal is not happening. You don't have to rebuff someone. Refusal is not an option.

Early Phase: You may start seeing signs of disapproval. A rejection may occur in the future. Someone may refuse to go along. The door may be slammed in your face. Your proposal may be rebuffed.

Late Phase: Rejection is no longer an issue. You're feeling less excluded. The period of disapproval is behind you. You're no longer concerned with dismissal.

Six of Pentacles

Upright

It's a time for issues of having/not having. You're involved with balancing resources, knowledge, or power. Questions of supply and demand are important.

Reversed

Keyword: Having/Not Having Resources

Absent: The distribution of resources is not a concern. You're not focused on getting more or having less. Who has what is not an issue. There's no need to think about supply.

Early Phase: You may have to think about resources in the future. You may need to take care of someone or be taken care of. A gift or reward may be offered. Issues of support may materialize.

Late Phase: There's less focus on resources. You no longer need to take care of someone or be taken care of. The time for a gift or reward is past. Support issues are decreasing.

Keyword: Having/Not Having Knowledge

Absent: The distribution of information is not a concern. You're not focused on what you know or don't know. You feel no need to offer or seek advice.

Early Phase: You may have to think about information in the future. You may start to teach or study. You may seek advice or be sought for your knowledge and opinion.

Late Phase: There's less focus on knowledge. The need to seek or offer advice is fading. You no longer want to teach or study. What people know is less important.

Keyword: Having/Not Having Power

Absent: The distribution of power is not a concern. You're not involved with who's in authority and who isn't. You're not coercing or being coerced.

Early Phase: You may have to think about power in the future. You may need to follow or lead. Issues of dominance and submission may become important.

Late Phase: There's less focus on power. The need to assert your authority or submit to someone is fading. Leadership issues are decreasing.

Seven of Pentacles

Upright

It's a time of assessment. You're taking stock of the situation. A reward is available. Your first efforts are bearing fruit. A direction change is in the air. A new path is worthy of consideration.

Reversed

Keyword: Assessment

Absent: No assessment is being made. There's no attempt to check results. You're not examining the situation closely. There's little time to pause and reflect.

Early Phase: You may need to evaluate. A status check may be coming up in the future. You may want to reassess where you're headed. A break may become necessary.

Late Phase: The assessment is ending. The time for evaluation is behind you. There's less need for thinking and planning. You no longer need to take stock of the situation.

Keyword: Reward

Absent: A reward is not materializing. There's no payoff at the moment. No sign of appreciation is appearing. You're not receiving your pat on the back.

Early Phase: A reward may be offered in the future. You may see some returns on your investment. A milestone may be coming up. A token of esteem may be presented.

Late Phase: The time for a reward has passed. Compensation is no longer available. The milestone is behind you. You've already received whatever was coming.

Keyword: Direction Change

Absent: A direction change is not happening. New opportunities are unavailable at the moment. You can't look at alternatives right now. A change of course is being blocked.

Early Phase: You may need a direction change in the future. Change may become more acceptable. A crossroads may be reached at some point. Someone may alter course.

Late Phase: The time for change is fading. The window of opportunity is closing. You're no longer weighing alternatives. A course adjustment is behind you.

Eight of Pentacles

Upright

It's a time of diligence. A great effort is being expended. A project is absorbing all your time. Knowledge is important. The information you want is available. You need to be careful and pay attention to detail.

Reversed

Keyword: Diligence

Absent: You're not working hard right now. A strong effort is not happening. You're not absorbed in a project. People are not industrious. No one is busy.

Early Phase: You may need to work harder in the future. A demanding project may be coming up. You may get involved in a new task. People may start gearing up for a big effort.

Late Phase: The hard work is behind you. You no longer need to work up a sweat. A project is winding down. Overtime is less available. You can slow down a bit.

Keyword: Knowledge

Absent: You're not pursuing knowledge. There's little opportunity to improve your skills. Research is not being done. You're having trouble getting the facts.

Early Phase: You may begin a course of study. You may need to increase your knowledge. School may become an option. An area of research may open up.

Late Phase: The time for study and learning is ending. A course is finishing. Your knowledge is decreasing. The research is nearing completion. You found out what you needed to know.

Keyword: Detail

Absent: There's little attention to detail. Someone is not being careful. The necessary checking is not being done. You're not handling all the loose ends.

Early Phase: Details may become important. People may start being more methodical. The need for monitoring may become clear. Care may be required in the future.

Late Phase: Extra care is no longer required. The need to check and double-check is past. You're less painstaking now. The detail work is ending.

Nine of Pentacles

Upright

It's a time of discipline. You need to control impulses and show restraint. Self-reliance is important. You can handle matters by yourself. An environment of refinement and gracious living is possible.

Reversed

Keyword: Discipline

Absent: There's little discipline at the moment. You're not sticking to the program. Wayward impulses are not being controlled. There's a lack of restraint.

Early Phase: You may need more discipline in the future. Self-control may become important. Someone may have to be restrained. A firm hand may be necessary.

Late Phase: Discipline is breaking down. Control measures are no longer in place. You're abandoning the program. People are less rigorous now. The regimen is no longer being followed.

Keyword: Self-Reliance

Absent: You can't act on your own. Your desire for independence is blocked. You can't handle the situation alone. Someone is not self-sufficient.

Early Phase: You may become more independent. You may be on your own in the future. Someone may become more self-reliant. You may need to break away at some point.

Late Phase: It's no longer possible to do everything yourself. A period of independence is ending. Being on your own is less satisfying now. The need for self-reliance is no longer strong.

Keyword: Refinement

Absent: There's a lack of refinement. People are not being tactful and polite. You're missing the finer things of life right now. Someone is refusing to be gracious.

Early Phase: People may become more courteous. You may seek more refined activities in the future. The environment may become more pleasant. There may be potential for gracious living.

Late Phase: People are no longer cordial. The gracious environment is disappearing. You're less interested in refined activities now. The gloves are coming off.

Ten of Pentacles

Upright

It's a time of affluence. All ventures are flourishing. Perma-
nence is important. A lasting foundation is being estab-
lished. People are following convention. There's a need to
comply with rules and guidelines.

Reversed

Keyword: Affluence

Absent: You're not enjoying abundance right now. Financial success is elusive.
You can't seem to get projects off the ground. Good fortune is
lacking.

Early Phase: Your fortunes may improve in the future. Your financial situation
may get better. Business may pick up. Some prospects may develop.

Late Phase: Your run of good fortune is ending. The prosperous times have
passed. You're no longer feeling financially secure. Business has taken a
turn for the worse.

Keyword: Permanence

Absent: You can't find a permanent solution. There's no solid base in place. No
one is focused on the long term. The family is not settled and secure.

Early Phase: You may seek a long-term solution. A more permanent foundation
may materialize. You may be able to settle down. A secure relationship
may become more appealing.

Late Phase: Your fixed arrangement is falling apart. You're no longer focused on
making the situation last. The mood of security is disappearing. A
long-lasting relationship is ending.

Keyword: Convention

Absent: There's little concern with convention. Traditions are not being followed. You don't trust the standard approach. Someone is not playing by the rules.

Early Phase: You may become more conservative. Rules may need to be followed. Someone may decide to go along with convention. A tradition may be honored.

Late Phase: You're no longer following a tradition. The mood is becoming less conventional. Known patterns are less effective. People are growing disenchanted with the old ways.

Page of Pentacles

Upright

Pentacles' energy is available to help you move in a new direction. The call to have an effect or be practical, prosperous, trusting, and trustworthy is strong right now. Take this chance to go beyond your usual limits and habits!

Reversed

Keywords: Have an Effect, Be Practical, Be Prosperous, Be Trusting/Trustworthy

Absent: The time is NOT right, or you CAN'T follow the call to:
put plans into motion, get heard, make physical changes, alter course, find a solution that works, use common sense, take advantage of what's available, get real, enrich yourself, enjoy abundance, reap rewards, make your fortune, keep your word, accept others at their word, stick by commitments, be credible.

Early Phase: The time MAY BE APPROACHING when you'll have a chance to:
achieve results, make a difference, set events in motion, realize your dream, work with what you have, be sensible, do what's necessary, accept reality, become secure, see your efforts flourish, attract you what you need, find the means, be dependable, have faith in someone, let go of the need to control, keep a promise.

Late Phase: The time is ENDING for any chance to:
work materially, take action, make an impression, apply pressure, solve a problem, be pragmatic, show good judgment, do what it takes, enjoy success, grow and expand, thrive, be comfortable, keep believing, stay loyal, honor your vow, stick to the agreement.

Knight of Pentacles

Upright

Pentacles' energy is extra strong. You, someone else, or the situation may be unwavering, cautious, thorough, realistic, and hardworking OR stubborn, unadventurous, obsessive, pessimistic, and grinding.

Reversed

Keywords (Positive): Unwavering, Cautious, Thorough, Realistic, Hardworking

Keywords (Negative): Stubborn, Unadventurous, Obsessive, Pessimistic, Grinding

Absent: You or someone else is NOT:

standing firm against opposition, staying true to convictions, showing caution, taking the prudent path, being thorough, covering all bases, facing the truth squarely, anticipating problems honestly, working hard, putting in a good effort OR being stubborn, refusing to listen to reason, being too conservative, settling for what's safe, being too picky, insisting on perfection, taking the gloomy view, dooming a project from the start, being humorless, driving others too hard.

Early Phase: You or another person MAY BEGIN to:

stay fixed to a course, be unwavering, check and double-check, proceed slowly, be meticulous, wrap up all loose ends, be willing to look at the facts, accept what's practical, tackle what needs doing, be industrious OR resist compromise, dig in to a position, be overly cautious, stay stuck in a rut, become obsessive, demand that everything be just so, be too pessimistic, concentrate on what's wrong, focus too much on work, forget about fun.

Late Phase: You or another person is NO LONGER:

refusing to quit, hanging in there, being careful, keeping eyes open, seeing the job through, taking care of the details, keeping feet on the ground, staying in the realm of possibility, staying productive, sticking to it OR impossible to budge, insisting on having his/her way, being a stick-in-the-mud, afraid to risk, nagging, being too compulsive, seeing the glass as half empty, focusing on the worst case, being a grind, cracking the whip.

Queen of Pentacles

Upright

Pentacles' energy is present as a state of being. A mood that is nurturing, bighearted, down-to-earth, resourceful, and trustworthy is evident. You or someone else is adopting or could adopt the mood of a parent, guardian, caretaker, nurturer, healer, friend, volunteer, resource person, confidante, or right-hand man.

Reversed

Keywords: Nurturing, Bighearted, Down-to-Earth, Resourceful, Trustworthy

Absent: The mood of you or someone else is NOT:
> supportive, nurturing, giving, generous, matter-of-fact, sensible, practical, handy, versatile, loyal, reliable.

Early Phase: The mood of you or someone else MAY BECOME:
> warm, natural, welcoming, abundant, unpretentious, simple, resourceful, ingenious, steadfast, trustworthy.

Late Phase: The mood of you or someone else is NO LONGER:
> loving in a practical way, sustaining, free of selfishness, bighearted, earthy, easygoing, pragmatic, workable, confidential, faithful.

King of Pentacles

Upright

Pentacles' energy is present in an active, outgoing way. Actions that are enterprising, adept, reliable, supporting, and steady are evident. You or someone else is acting or could act as a businessperson, entrepreneur, manager, deal-maker, problem-solver, craftsperson, artisan, provider, philanthropist, or source of strength.

Reversed

Keywords: Enterprising, Adept, Reliable, Supporting, Steady

Absent: You or someone else is NOT:

> enterprising, attracting wealth, showing competence, using skills, meeting commitments, assuming responsibility, offering to help, providing support, remaining constant, keeping regular habits.

Early Phase: You or someone else MAY BEGIN to:

> make something work, solve the problem, prove adept, focus on what's practical, keep promises, stay reliable, give generously, encourage someone, provide stability, work steadily toward a goal.

Late Phase: You or someone else is NO LONGER:

> picking up on opportunities, taking care of business, managing well, relying on experts, instilling trust, following through, giving time and attention, propping up, staying calm, avoiding mood swings.

To Our Readers

Weiser Books, an imprint of Red Wheel/Weiser, publishes books across the entire spectrum of occult, esoteric, speculative, and New Age subjects. Our mission is to publish quality books that will make a difference in people's lives without advocating any one particular path or field of study. We value the integrity, originality, and depth of knowledge of our authors.

Our readers are our most important resource, and we appreciate your input, suggestions, and ideas about what you would like to see published.

Visit our website at *www.redwheelweiser.com*, where you can learn about our upcoming books and free downloads, and also find links to sign up for our newsletter and exclusive offers.

You can also contact us at *info@rwwbooks.com* or at

Red Wheel/Weiser, LLC
65 Parker Street, Suite 7
Newburyport, MA 01950